Aviation and Space
Science Projects

Aviation and Space Science Projects

Dr. Ben Millspaugh

TAB **TAB BOOKS**
Blue Ridge Summit, PA

NOTICES

Elmer's Glue   Borden Company
Silver Star Sleeper   Silver Star Systems, Inc.
Model Master   Testor's Company

FIRST EDITION
SECOND PRINTING

Library of Congress Cataloging-in-Publication Data

Millspaugh, Ben P.
    Aviation and space science projects / by Ben Millspaugh.
       p. cm.
    Includes index.
    Summary: Includes projects dealing with air density, wind, balloons, gliders, spacecraft, and many more aviation and space -related categories.
    ISBN 0-8306-2157-1 (h)   ISBN 0-8306-2156-3 (p)
    1. Aeronautics—Experiments—Juvenile literature. 2. Space sciences—Experiments—Juvenile literature. [1. Aeronautics--Experiments 2. Space sciences—Experiments. 3. Science projects] I. Title.
TL547.M63 1991   91-25830
507'.8—dc20   CIP
                                              AC

TAB Books offers software for sale. For information and a catalog, please contact TAB Software Department, Blue Ridge Summit, PA 17294-0850.

Acquisitions Editor: Kimberly Tabor
Director of Production: Katherine G. Brown
Book Design: Jaclyn J. Boone
Cover Design and Illustration: Greg Schooley, Mars, Pennsylvania   AV1

Contents

Resources   111

Glossary   125

Index   131

To three people who have had a tremendous impact upon my aerospace education career:

Bill Mitchell was my first flight instructor and he made me believe that I really could fly an airplane.

A. Scott Crossfield, one of the great pioneers in aerospace. He presented me with the Aerospace Teacher of the Year Award for 1989, which was the greatest moment in my career.

Helen Frizzell opened my eyes to the potential of aerospace education and how it could be used to excite the minds of young people.

Acknowledgments

The author would like to thank those individuals who helped make this book a reality.

I thank Eulah Gibson, Dawn Ragain, Mike Terpenning, and Kevin Sagar for being student models in the projects. Dawn Ragain built and flew the majority of the projects. They demonstrated the potential in every student when exploring air and space sciences.

I would like to acknowledge Dave Binkendorf of McDonnell-Douglas for his help in getting clearance to use the artwork of the National Aerospace Plane and the National Project Office.

Scott Skinner provided valuable input about the fascinating world of kite technology.

Thanks go to Richard Swetlik for his information about parachutes and to Annie Pyrne who assembled information and photographs on airships.

I wish to thank the representatives of several companies that granted permission to reprint excerpts from their publications: Frank Mitchell, Beech Aircraft Corporation; Russ Watson, Cessna Aircraft Company Air Age Education; Gen. Carl Miller and Hal Bacon, Civil Air Patrol; and Bob Cannon, Estes Industries. These individuals are leaders in the field of aerospace education and their help in making this book a reality is most appreciated.

Introduction

AVIATION AND SPACE SCIENCE PROJECTS is designed for the young person interested in aviation and spaceflight. It is not just a book of fun things to build, it is a learning experience for the young person.

The book is broken down into chapters that cover the different categories of aircraft and spacecraft. If you want to be a pilot or astronaut someday, you will start your training in one of the categories covered in this book. Some people start by learning to fly a sailplane (glider); others, in a hot-air balloon; others in an airplane or helicopter.

Aviation and Space Science Projects is especially helpful to teachers who want to learn more about aerospace. An appendix of resources will help students and teachers obtain more information. Resources are listed for information about the many facets of aviation and spaceflight. The book is designed to be a supplement for aerospace education workshop teachers.

When building any of the projects shown, the reader should take every precaution for safety. Adult supervision is recommended both in building and flying a project. Follow the safety recommendations closely and you will not only build a fun project, it will be safe.

I sincerely hope this book will help you along the way if you are interested in a career in aerospace. I have tried to make it interesting for every young person. The wonderful world of aerospace needs you and you are its future.

Welcome aboard!
Dr. Ben Millspaugh

Safety checklist

CHECKLISTS ARE REQUIRED for safe air and space travel. Engineers, technicians, pilots, and astronauts rely on step-by-step reminders to ensure that everything is functioning properly before continuing to the next activity; an engineer or technician follows a prescribed start-up and shutdown procedure to simply move an aircraft from one corner of an airport to the opposite corner; a pilot follows checklists to start engines, taxi, prepare for takeoff, take off, cruise, approach, and landing; likewise, an astronaut relies on a checklist for each phase of a mission; and emergency procedures for aircraft and spacecraft are specifically spelled out and practiced time and again, each time relying on a prescribed checklist.

This book is an ideal opportunity to explore the importance of checklists in aerospace with hands-on experience; therefore, this checklist shall help the student (and teacher) work in a safe environment—reducing stress on participants—while improving the chances for successful execution and completion of the project or experiment.

Refer to this checklist whenever you see the stop sign: 🛑

- ☞ Review this checklist to determine which items apply to the task, then follow through on those checklist items to be safe. Verify the appropriate selections with an adult.
- ☞ Never work alone.
- ☞ Adult supervision.
- ☞ Remove all jewelry.
- ☞ Tie up loose hair and loose clothing.
- ☞ Use proper safety equipment: gloves, safety glasses, an apron, and the like.
- ☞ Follow each step, never perform shortcuts.
- ☞ Taste nothing that is not directly food related.
- ☞ Check location of first aid kit and fire extinguisher.
- ☞ Beware of chemicals: use with care; proper ventilation; clean up spills as soon as safely possible; follow the product's printed instructions.

☞ Clean up broken glass as soon as safely possible with a dust pan and brush.

☞ Use common sense. Before proceeding to the next step, consider the outcome of that step to ensure safety.

☞ Clean up the work area and properly dispose of waste.

☞ Clean and properly store any tools, brushes, paints, and the like, that have been used for the project.

☞ Wash hands upon completion of the project or experiment. Wash hands during the project, if necessary.

☞ Review this checklist upon completion of the project to make sure everything is in order.

1

The flight environment

IF YOU WERE GOING TO LEARN how to sail a boat, you would eventually have to know something about water, maybe even the ocean. The same holds true for aircraft. If you are going to learn about aircraft, you should have an understanding of the air (Fig. 1-1).

Fig. 1-1.

THE ATMOSPHERE AND ITS STRUCTURE

There is an ocean of air around the earth called the *atmosphere*. It starts at the ground and goes up to the edge of space. Scientists have found that the atmosphere is made up of layers. The first layer is known as the *troposphere*. It starts at the surface of the earth and goes up to about eight miles high.

In your science classes at school, your teacher might have mentioned a layer called the *tropopause*. This is a layer that separates the troposphere and the next layer above it, known as the *stratosphere*. The stratosphere goes up to an altitude of about 22 miles. Nearly 99 percent of the earth's atmosphere is below this 22 miles. At an altitude of 22 miles, it isn't a very friendly place. There isn't much oxygen. For a pilot or astronaut to live at this altitude, he or she must have additional oxygen.

The middle portion of the stratosphere has been in the news recently. It is commonly referred to as the *ozone layer*. We humans are destroying part of it by using too many chemicals, called *fluorocarbons*. (Fluorocarbons are found in certain spray cans and fire extinguishers. You can help save our environment by not using products that contain harmful fluorocarbons. If you don't know what products are harmful, ask your science teacher at school.)

The next layer is the *mesosphere*, and above that is the *thermosphere*, also called the *ionosphere*. At the upper limit, the *exosphere* becomes *outer space* somewhere between 500 to 1,000 miles above the earth's surface.

Air is a mixture

Air is a gas and is made up of several elements. This mixture consists of approximately 79 percent nitrogen, 19 percent oxygen, and another 2 percent of assorted gases. This 2 percent includes carbon dioxide, argon, neon, and helium. When you take in a deep breath of air, you are getting mostly nitrogen. Normally nitrogen is invisible; however, there is a way to see it. It has to be so cold it becomes a liquid. This is known as liquid nitrogen.

🛑 Experimenting with liquid nitrogen

An adult should be in charge of this experiment. You might ask your science teacher at school to do it for the whole class. It is fun and educational. Nitrogen is available through companies that specialize in liquid gases.

Liquid nitrogen comes in a container called a Dewar flask (Fig. 1-2). Nitrogen is extremely cold and becomes a liquid at −320°F. Oxygen, the other main part of air, becomes a liquid at −297°F. (Caution: Liquid oxygen is very explosive. Do not attempt to experiment with it under any circumstances.) The Dewar flask is much like a large vacuum storage bottle that keeps the liquid nitrogen cold for long periods of time.

Teacher Roger Bartholomew helps student Mike Terpenning pour the liquid nitrogen into a coffee can (Fig. 1-3). Notice that both are wearing protective glasses and gloves; if the liquid nitrogen were to get into the eyes or onto the

Fig. 1-2. Liquid nitrogen comes in a vacuum bottle container called a Dewar flask, which keeps the liquid nitrogen cold for a long time.

skin, it would cause permanent damage. Just to show how cold liquid nitrogen is, Mike sticks a banana into the liquid (Fig. 1-4). It freezes the banana so hard Mike can use it to drive a nail into a piece of pine board (Fig. 1-5).

Other interesting things can be done with liquid nitrogen. If you put a piece of lettuce in it, the leaf becomes so hard it will shatter like glass. Students like to watch the cloud form when tap water is poured into the cold liquid (Fig. 1-6).

Air does contain a small amount of water in vapor form. It might be as low as one percent in some desert areas, and up to five percent near the ocean. When the temperature of the air reaches the point where water vapor begins to become visible, a cloud might form. The temperature at which clouds form is called the *dew point*.

🛑 Experimenting with the weight of air

Air does have weight, which can be proven in an experiment.

The experiment requires some string, a yardstick, and two balloons. First inflate the two balloons and try to make them exactly the same size. Student Dawn Ragain ties off the ends so that no air will escape (Fig. 1-7). Make sure the strings are of equal length. A loop is made in the string. Each balloon is tied with its own piece of string. The balloons are then suspended from each end of the

Fig. 1-3. Teacher Roger Bartholomew helps student Mike Terpenning pour the liquid nitrogen into a coffee can. Both are wearing protective glasses and gloves.

Fig. 1-4. Mike sticks a banana into the liquid.

Fig. 1-5. The banana freezes so hard that Mike can use it to drive a nail into a piece of pine board.

Fig. 1-6. A cloud forms when ordinary tap water is poured into the liquid nitrogen. Nitrogen-frozen lettuce leaves become so brittle that they shatter like glass.

Fig. 1-7. Student Dawn Ragain ties off the balloon ends so that no air will escape. Each balloon is tied with its own piece of string.

yardstick (Fig. 1-8). If you tie another string at the center of the yardstick, it should balance. Each balloon will hang from the ends of the yardstick. Note that Dawn is wearing eye protection. When a balloon bursts, pieces can fly off in all directions. It is always a good idea to protect your eyes from this danger.

If you have done it right, the balloons will be about the same distance from the center of the yardstick. You can move the balloons back and forth until they balance. We are now ready to burst one of the balloons.

Fig. 1-8. The balloons are then suspended from each end of a yardstick, which is balanced by another string at the center. Dawn is wearing eye protection because when a balloon bursts, pieces might fly off in all directions.

Fig. 1-9. The broken balloon should remain intact, without disintegrating, to show that the remaining balloon is heavier. If the broken balloon does disintegrate, do it again with less balloon inflation because overinflation encourages disintegration.

Before we start the countdown, make sure the yardstick is balanced. You can do this by moving the center string back and forth. Is everything balanced? Good. Using a straight pin, let's pop one of the balloons. The countdown is on: Three—Two— One—BANG! Now what do you see? The remaining balloon is heavier (Fig. 1-9). When the other balloon bursts, it should remain intact. If it does not, do it again and try not to fill up the balloons quite so much. The more that they are inflated, the greater the chances of tearing.

Air is made up of zillions of tiny molecules all moving around and bouncing up against one another. When it is really cold, the molecules are slow and do not bounce quite as much. On the other hand, when they are hot, they really get active and bounce against one another a lot more.

AIR DENSITY

The number of air molecules in a given volume is known as the *air density*. Imagine a giant balloon. This balloon is about 10 miles long, 10 miles wide, and 10 miles high. Let's say that there is a huge door where you could enter. Imagine that you were a pilot in an airplane and you could go right inside that balloon and then take off and fly inside it.

Okay, there is only so much air inside the balloon. If you made the air inside the giant balloon really cold, the airplane would fly much better. On the other hand, if you made the air inside the giant balloon hot, the airplane wouldn't fly nearly as well. When the air is cold, it is thicker. When the air is thicker, or more dense, airplanes fly better. When the air is warm, it gets thinner, or less dense.

If the giant balloon were placed on the moon where there is no air, the airplane wouldn't fly at all because it takes air molecules to make an airplane fly. The more molecules, the better it flies. When air is cold, there are more molecules, and airplanes like that.

AIR DRAG

Drag is the resistance of the air to anything that moves through it. For example, when you walk waist-deep through a swimming pool, you notice that it is difficult to go fast. That is because the water is working against you. This resistance is known as drag. When an object tries to move through air, drag occurs. Air works against that object. A perfect example of an object that uses this principle to slow it down is a parachute. When a parachute is opened, it creates more drag and this allows the human jumper to descend slow enough to allow a safe landing on the earth.

Parachutes

Basically, it works like this: A skydiver goes up to a high altitude in an airplane and jumps out. Gravity pulls the person toward the ground and a device, called a parachute, slows the person to a safe speed for landing. Upon leaving the aircraft, a jumper pulls a cord and out pops the parachute (Fig. 1-10).

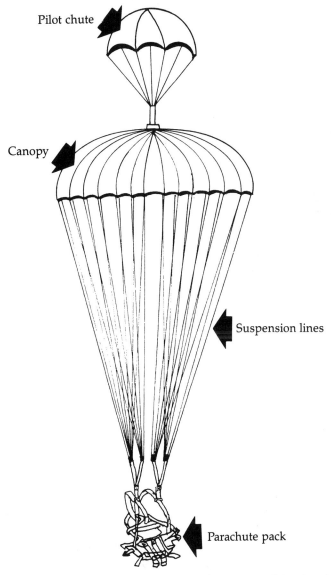

Fig. 1-10. A standard parachute is designed to use the drag energy of the air to bring a jumper safely back to earth.

A *pilot chute* is a small parachute attached to the top of the canopy. The pilot chute pulls the *canopy* from the pack. The canopy is the large umbrella-like area of nylon cloth that slows the jumper. The *suspension lines* connect the canopy to the harness. The *pack* is the assembly that encloses the pilot chute, the canopy, and suspension lines. The *harness* is an arrangement of nylon webbing and metal fittings that is worn by the jumper and can provide a seat during descent. The device that trips or releases the parachute is called a *rip cord*.

Interesting facts about parachutes

- History's first recorded idea of a parachute was made by Leonardo da Vinci in the year 1495.
- The first parachute jump was in France. A man by the name of LeHormand, tested a "life-belt" on December 26, 1783. It was a cone-shaped device, 14 feet in diameter, with a wicker frame. He made the jump off the Montpelier Observatory after first testing the chute with various weights.
- The first jump from a balloon was by R. Jordarki Kaparaut at Warsaw, Poland, in 1808 because his balloon caught fire. (The first recorded aerial deaths occurred during an attempt to cross the English Channel in 1795. Two balloonists, Pilatre de Rozier and M. Romain, were killed when their balloon caught fire.)
- The first jump from an airplane, was made on March 1, 1912, by Captain Albert Berry of Jefferson Barracks, Missouri, from an altitude of 1,500 feet.

RELATIVE WIND

To understand how airplanes, gliders, and helicopters fly, you must know something about the forces of air and how the air's energy can lift an aircraft away from the earth.

Air is an invisible gas and unless you feel it, or see it in a container like a balloon, it is difficult to realize that air is present. Although air is invisible, you can see its presence, especially with high wind or when a storm has passed. Air contains energy and an aircraft captures, or harnesses, part of that energy when it flies.

You can harness part of that energy when you put your hand out the window of a car and let it "ski" along as the car is moving forward. The air that is moving is called wind, and if it is moving in a direction opposite to your hand, it is called the *relative wind* (Fig. 1-11).

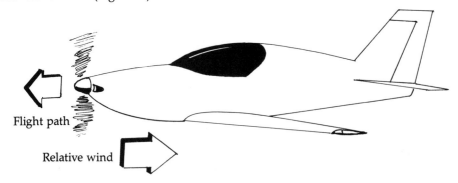

Fig. 1-11. Relative wind is the flow of air that moves opposite the flight path of an aircraft.

2

Birds, balloons, and blimps

EARLY MAN THOUGHT THAT FLIGHT WAS ONLY FOR GODS, or angels, or birds. He tried to fly by making wings of feathers. These attempts failed and it was not until the eighteenth century that man achieved success. One of the earliest recorded stories of man's attempt to fly occurred in ancient Greece.

THE FLIGHT OF ICARUS AND DAEDALUS

According to Greek mythology, a father and his son were the first to fly. The father's name was Daedalus. The son's name was Icarus. The two had been imprisoned and they knew the only way to escape was to fly. The prison was located on an island and it was about 70 miles to the nearest land.

The father and son collected seabird feathers and beeswax from inside the prison. These were carefully concealed from the prison guards. When time came for their escape, they worked all night making wings for their arms. At dawn the next morning, the two men climbed up onto the walls of the prison while the guards slept. The wings were attached to their arms. As they began to move their arms up and down, they flew out toward the sea and away from the prison.

The father warned his son not to fly too high because the sun might melt the wax. The wax held the feathers in place. Icarus, the son, was so excited about the freedom of flying that he didn't listen to his father (Fig. 2-1). As Icarus flew higher and higher, the wax on his wings started to melt. They came apart and he crashed to his death in the sea near an island that now bears his name.

Daedalus flew on to Sicily where he lived a long life of freedom. Keep in mind that this story was only a myth; however, it was one of the first stories of early man's dream to conquer flight.

THE FIRST SUCCESSFUL AIRCRAFT WAS A BIRD

A bird is a magnificent flying machine. Every system in a bird is designed for the task of flying. For example, notice the legs. A bird has small feet and legs—compare that to an airplane. The airplane has "small feet and legs" and huge wings.

Fig. 2-1. Icarus   Beech Aircraft Corporation

A bird is light; an airplane is light (in relation to its ability to fly). The idea is to keep everything as light as possible; therefore, both the bird and the airplane follow the same pattern.

When a bird flies, it first lifts its wings upward. This prepares for the all-important downstroke. Then, as the powerful muscles in the back and shoulders pull the wings downward, the lifting stroke occurs. As the wing moves downward, it pulls the relative wind over the feathers and this creates *lift* (Fig. 2-2). Once the lift stroke is near the bottom—where the wing tips are pointed downward—the body responds by moving upward. The wind passing over the bird's body, opposite its flight path, is called the relative wind, just like an airplane (Fig. 2-3).

Some birds are very fast. One of the fastest in straight flight is a swift. In a dive, a peregrine falcon can exceed 100 mph. Scientists have used radar guns to clock the speed of birds.

Leonardo da Vinci, a famous Italian artist, sculptor, and designer, was the first person known to dream up several flying devices. (Recall that he came up with the concept of a parachute.) One of his lesser-known, yet historical designs was an ornithopter, an aircraft that flaps its wings.

🛑 Experimenting with the ornithopter

An ornithopter is a flapping wing mechanical aircraft. One of the most successful ornithopter toys is called the Flying Bird (Fig. 2-4). (For the address of where to get a Flying Bird, see the resources appendix). This outstanding toy is an excellent flyer and will give hours of enjoyment. All you have to do is wind up

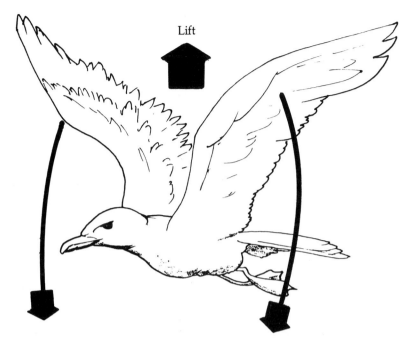

Fig. 2-2. A bird's wings in this position are ready to pull downward, which creates lift.

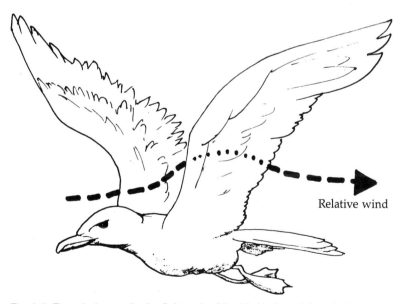

Fig. 2-3. The wind opposite the fight path of the bird is the relative wind.

Fig. 2-4. Flying Bird is an extremely successful ornithopter toy that combines hours of fun with an educational experience.

the rubber band and let it fly (Figs. 2-5 and 2-6). It is different than most model aircraft in that it is noisy. It is best to fly it outside or in an area where mom won't be upset by the racket it makes. By moving the tail feathers, the Flying Bird can make turns, dives, rolls, and other maneuvers. If you like birds, you'll love Flying Bird.

Fig. 2-5. Wind it up.

Additionally, if you enjoy watching birds flying, here is a toy that actually "flies" when the wind blows. It is a wooden duck (Fig. 2-7) that has nylon cords supporting its wings, much like a mobile. There is a counterweight on the bottom of the bird's body. This makes the wings flap smoothly when a breeze is encountered. Speciality shops, such as Into the Wind (*see* appendix), carry these for fewer than $20.

Fig. 2-6. Let it fly.

Fig. 2-7. This wooden duck mobile flies when the wind, the breeze from a fan, or an air-conditioning vent hits it. A counterweight on the bottom of the bird's body makes the wings flap smoothly in a breeze.

THE BALLOON

The first man-made "aircraft" to actually fly was a hot-air balloon. Two French brothers, by the name of Montgolfier, are credited with developing the first successful flying balloon device. On November 21, 1783, a French doctor and a military officer took off and flew around Paris for about 25 minutes (Fig. 2-8). (A rooster, a duck, and a sheep flew before the humans.)

Fig. 2-8. Montgolfier's balloon.

🛑 Experimenting with a hot-air balloon

You can make a hot-air balloon that flies beautifully. The balloon is made of tissue paper and wire. It works on the principle of *buoyancy*. Here's how:

Imagine that you have two containers of air that are exactly the same size. If the air in one container is warm and the air in the other container is cold, the warm-air container is lighter. If you filled a large balloon (one container) with a lot of warm (lightweight) air, the balloon would start to rise. A balloon large enough and strong enough could lift one or more humans.

To build a hot-air balloon, you will need some tissue paper, glue, a piece of wire, and a heating source. You can also buy a beautiful kit from Space Age Products that shall be used for this experiment. (*See* Space Age Products' address in appendix.)

The hot-air balloon kit contains 15 precut panels of grade 1 tissue paper. There is wire for the bottom ring and a cord for tying off the top of the balloon. A white glue, such as Elmer's, is recommended.

1. Select two different color panels. Lay one on top of the other as shown in the photograph. Allow a one-half inch margin to show on the bottom panel (Fig. 2-9).

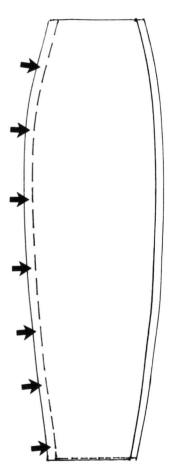

Fig. 2-9. The first step of making a balloon is to lay one panel on top of the other.

2. Apply a thin line of glue to the half-inch margin on the bottom of panel #1. Fold this over the edge of panel #2 (Fig. 2-10).

Fig. 2-10. Apply a thin line of glue to the half-inch margin.

3. Place panel #3 on top of panel #2 allowing a half-inch margin to show on panel #2 on the unglued side (Fig. 2-11). Repeat gluing as in step #2 (Fig. 2-12).

Fig. 2-11. Place panel #3 on top of panel #2.   Fig. 2-12. Repeat gluing.

4. Paste the remaining 12 panels using this method.
5. Join the free edges of panel #1 to panel #5 as shown on the end view of panels (Fig. 2-13).

Fig. 2-13. Glue the panels as shown. Free edges of the first and last panel are glued together making a complete enclosure.

6. After gluing, carefully separate all folds to keep them from sticking together.

7. Tie off the top of the balloon. Leave a loop in the cord for holding the balloon up while inflating.
8. Open the hole in the bottom of the balloon and make a wire ring to fit the hole. Place the ring inside the opening and fold paper approximately one inch over it. Glue the paper that is over the wire into place (Fig. 2-14).

Fig. 2-14. Open the hole in the bottom of the balloon and install a wire ring that fits the hole.

9. Let the glue dry for about two hours. You may test-inflate the balloon with a fan or a reversed vacuum cleaner to blow air. Loose edges and small dime-size holes should not make much difference (Fig. 2-15). You may make major repairs with glue and paper. You may even stand inside the balloon to make repairs. When repairs are done, you are ready for launching.

Fig. 2-15. Let the balloon dry for about two hours. Test-inflate the balloon with a fan.

During the launch, you will need the help of an adult and at least two friends. (The adult should read the complete hot-air balloon section, plus instructions with the kit for proper knowledge of the experiment, related equipment, and safety precautions.) You do not want to set the balloon on fire, so take care during inflation.

There are several ways to build the heater. One way is to use a garage heater, sometimes called a *salamander* (Fig. 2-16), which is fueled by kerosene. The salamander will provide the most heat in the shortest time. The heater can be rented from a local rental store.

Fig. 2-16. One way to inflate the balloon is to use a garage heater.

Another source of heat can be obtained from a hardware store. You will need to purchase a length of stove pipe that is about 4 feet long and about 6 inches in diameter. The stove pipe should have an elbow just about in the middle.

You might use burning paper as a fuel. One of the problems with burning paper is the ashen pieces that might rise up into the balloon; therefore, the end that inflates the balloon should have a wire screen covering it so that pieces of burning paper do not fly up into the balloon. A door has to be made at the opposite end of the stove pipe. This door allows you to insert paper that can be burned.

Another kind of fuel is known as Sterno. This is a canned, solid, alcohol fuel that is commonly used in camp stoves. If you want to use Sterno, you may make a shorter stovepipe, but with a larger diameter. The stovepipe may be shortened to 1 to 2 feet long. It is recommended that you use stovepipe that is 10 inches in diameter.

You are ready to launch. Ideal launch conditions usually occur in the early morning or late evening with little or no wind. It is recommended that the balloon not be launched in a breeze because of a possible fire hazard. Sand or bricks may be piled around the bottom of the stovepipe for support.

To inflate the balloon, have a friend hold the top of the balloon with a pole that has a string with one end tied to the end of the pole and the other end of the string tied to the balloon. The adult helping you will hold the balloon over the opening of the stove pipe heater. You or a friend may handle the heat source, whether garage heater, newspaper, or Sterno, under the watchful eye of the adult. Have your crumpled paper handy so you can keep a steady supply of fuel to the burner.

If you are using Sterno, put it inside the pipe and light it. You will need to have a source of ventilation. Make sure that the Sterno has space at the bottom of the can to get air.

Caution: The paper balloon naturally will burn if ignited. If the balloon catches fire, especially if you're using paper as a fuel, do not try to extinguish the balloon. Let the balloon rise; the fire will consume the balloon.

As stated earlier, the safest heat source is the garage heater. It is worth the extra effort to rent or borrow one for the heat source. The second best source of heat is the Sterno. However, Sterno and paper create open flames and precautions must be taken to prevent flames from reaching the balloon.

Finally, it is recommended that you launch in an open area. A school yard, empty playground, or large park is best. Let your adult helper pick what they think is a good place.

When the balloon stands up by itself, it is ready to fly. The person holding the pole at the top of the balloon may untie the cord from the balloon. The person holding the balloon at the mouth of the heater will feel the tug because the balloon wants to fly.

Consider using lightweight heat-resistant cord to tether the balloon prior to launch. Perhaps you could tie a short section of the cord to opposite sides of the wire frame at the bottom, then tie a longer section of cord—essentially a kite string arrangement—at the center of that section to control the balloon.

At this point, it may be released.

The balloon will take off and fly. If the inside of the balloon is quite warm, and it is a cool, perhaps a cold day outside, the balloon will really take off and fly (Fig. 2-17). The balloon might go quite a distance if untethered. The greater the temperature difference between the balloon and the outside air, the better. This creates more buoyancy. One of the nicest things about a hot-air balloon is that it can be launched again and again, as long as it lands safely and as long as you have fuel for the heater.

Fig. 2-17. The balloon will take off and fly.

A MODERN HOT-AIR BALLOON

A balloon operates on the principle of buoyancy. Because hot air is lighter than cold air, it will rise. If this hot air can be contained, the container will rise. The large container of a balloon is called an *envelope*. Attached to the envelope are strong lines that support a *gondola* (*basket*) (Fig. 2-18). The pilot and passengers

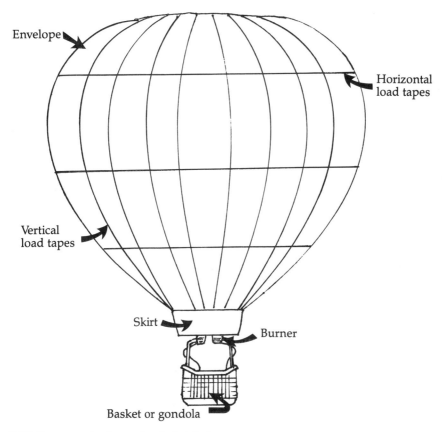

Fig. 2-18. Components of a modern hot-air balloon.

ride in the gondola. Fuel for the burner that produces the hot air is also in the gondola (Fig. 2-19). The fuel is usually propane gas. When the pilot pulls on a cord attached to a smaller burner, large amounts of propane enter the larger burner and instantly ignites. Hot air from the flames rises into the envelope. The hot air trapped in the envelope lifts the weight of the envelope, gondola, passengers, and other apparatuses into the air (Fig. 2-20).

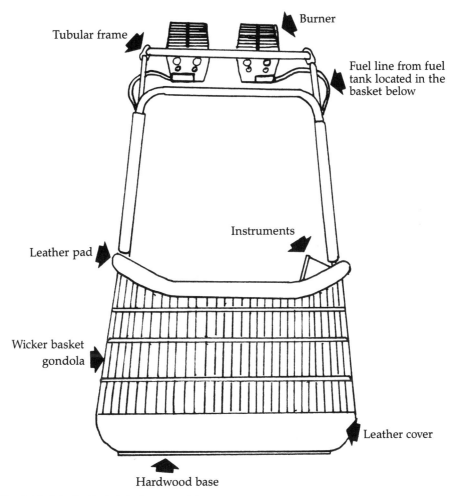

Fig. 2-19. A typical hot-air balloon gondola.

Questions and answers about balloons

Question: How do you steer a balloon?

Answer: You don't! You might find an altitude where the winds are blowing in the preferred direction and hope that the balloon goes that direction.

Question: How high does a balloon go?

Answer: Hot-air balloons have gone over 50,000 feet high.

Fig. 2-20. Flames from the burner produce the hot air that is trapped in the envelope. The hot air causes the balloon to rise, carrying the gondola and passengers.

Question: How long can a balloon stay up?

Answer: Most balloons can stay up for 1-2 hours. This depends upon the fuel carried and the outside temperature.

Question: How fast does a balloon go?

Answer: As fast as the wind.

Question: What does it take to be a pilot?

Answer: Balloon pilots must have training and be certificated by the Federal Aviation Administration. Training includes ground school and flight instruction, followed by a flight test with a certificated examiner.

Question: How does a balloon return to the airport if you cannot steer it?

Answer: A *chase crew* in a vehicle, typically a pickup truck, follows the balloon and commonly communicates with the pilot on a radio. Once the balloon lands, it can be packed into a small space and placed in the back of the pickup or on a trailer for the trip to its normal storage spot at home or at the airport.

Question: How big is a balloon?

Answer: The average balloon is about 70 feet high and has a diameter of about 50 feet. It holds about 57,000 cubic feet of hot air. The largest balloons might have as much as 140,000 cubic feet of capacity.

Question: What is a balloon made of?

Answer: The envelope is made of about 1,000 square yards of reinforced nylon fabric called *rip-stop*. It is extremely light and very strong. It doesn't burn easily and is made so that it will not easily tear.

Question: What is a balloon filled with?

Answer: The most popular balloons are filled with hot air from the flames of a burner. Others might be filled with helium.

Question: What fuel is burned to make the air hot?

Answer: Propane gas is the most common fuel carried on the balloon. The pressurized propane is routed to the burner through hoses. Flames might shoot up as far as six to eight feet in a wide, open blast. The balloon pilot controls this flame.

Question: How does a balloon work?

Answer: Hot air rises. The envelope traps a large bubble of hot air. When enough hot air from the burner's flame is trapped in the envelope, the balloon rises. If the air in the envelope is allowed to cool, or escape, the balloon will descend.

Question: How much does a balloon weigh?

Answer: A typical balloon weighs approximately 500 pounds. In the air, the complete system, including the hot air, might weigh as much as 2.5 tons.

Question: How much does a balloon cost?

Answer: The average balloon costs between $12,000 and $25,000. This price includes the envelope, gondola, fuel tanks, instruments, and other apparatus.

ZEPPELINS

One problem when flying a balloon is the lack of directional control. This means that once the balloon leaves the ground, it is subject to the wind and wherever the wind wants to take it.

In the late 1800s, airmen started experimenting with balloons that could be controlled. The balloons were known as *airships* and they had control surfaces that included a rudder and an elevator. The airships were powered by engine-driven propellers.

One of the great airship designers was Germany's Ferdinand von Zeppelin. Because they were some of the greatest airships of all time, in Europe the word Zeppelin is spoken instead of airship.

A little trivia concerning the name Zeppelin: Your parents or grandparents might tell you that when something was a failure, it is said to, "...go over like a lead balloon." This means that a balloon made of the heavy metal lead would not fly. In Europe, they said, "...it goes over like a lead Zeppelin." This is where the name for the rock group Led Zeppelin originated.

One of von Zeppelin's greatest achievements was an airship known as *Hindenburg*. It was slightly longer than three football fields placed end to end and it was filled with highly explosive hydrogen gas, rather than inert helium. This huge flying machine exploded while *mooring* (airships land by being attached to a tower and reeled into the tower) at the naval base near Lakehurst, New Jersey, in 1937. It was the end of all Zeppelin operations.

BLIMPS

It is equally correct to refer to a blimp as a *dirigible*. By definition, a dirigible is a lighter-than-air craft that is engine driven and steerable. A Zeppelin is only a rigid airship.

The Goodyear Tire & Rubber Company has built more than 300 blimps since 1917. The name blimp came from the English Navy officer Lt. A.D. Cunningham. He was conducting an airship inspection and reached up and flipped his thumb at the gas bag and a strange noise came from the fabric. Lt. Cunningham smiled, then imitated the sound his thumb made on the fabric: "Blimp!"

Airships are either *rigid* or *nonrigid*. Rigid airships have metal frameworks within the envelope to keep their shape. Nonrigid models maintain shape by the internal pressure of the helium gas aided by air cells called *ballonets*. Goodyear blimps are nonrigid airships (Fig. 2-21).

COMPONENTS OF AN AIRSHIP

1. Nose Cone Battens (supports)
2. Forward Ballonet (air bag inside envelope)
3. Catenary Curtain and Suspension Cables (inside envelope)
4. Aft Ballonet
5. Control Surfaces (rudders and elevators)
6. Car—Passenger Compartment
7. Engines
8. Night Sign Lamps
9. Air Scoops (channel air to ballonets)
10. Air Valves (regulate air in ballonets)
11. Helium Valve

Goodyear Tire & Rubber Company

VITAL STATISTICS

Overall Dimensions:		Power:		Envelope Fabric:	
Length	192 feet	Twin Continental Engines	210 hp. each	Material (2-ply)	Rubber-coated
Height	59 feet	(6 cylinders, pusher type)			Polyester Fabric
Width	50 feet	Cruising Speed	35 mph.		
Volume	202,700 cubic feet	Maximum Speed	50 mph.	**Night Sign:**	"Super Skytacular"
				Number of lights	7,560 (total
Weight and Lift:		**Operational Limits:**			both sides)
Maximum Gross Weight	12,320 lbs.	Normal Altitude	1,000-3,000 feet	Height of Sign	24.5 feet
Weight Empty	9,500 lbs.	Maximum Altitude	10,000 feet	Length of Sign	105 feet
Maximum Lift	2,820 lbs.	Range	500 miles	Amount of Wiring	80 miles
No. of Passengers	Six plus pilot			Readability	1 mile
				Colors	Red, Green, Blue, Yellow

Fig. 2-21. Airships are rigid and nonrigid. Airships with metal frameworks inside the envelope to maintain the shape are rigid; nonrigid airship shape is maintained by the internal pressure of the helium lifting gas aided by ballonets. The Goodyear blimps are nonrigid airships.

Goodyear built two giant rigid airships for the Navy in the 1930s. Unfortunately, both were lost in storms after two years of service. Goodyear built a series of large observation blimps in the 1940s and 1950s that were used to protect Naval fleets along the coast. Some of these airships could stay aloft for longer than a week. The endurance record of an airship is 11 days.

Goodyear operates several airships in the United States: (among them) *America*, based in Houston; *Columbia*, based in Los Angeles; and *Enterprise*, based in Pompano Beach, Florida (Fig. 2-22).

Fig. 2-22. Two airships operated by Goodyear are moored at one airport.

3

Primitive gliders, hang gliders, kites, and sailplanes

GREAT AVIATION PIONEERS came from all over the world: Sir George Cayley was English; Otto Lilienthal was German; and the Wright brothers were American. Perhaps you would like to better understand the international flavor of aviation by making an easy paper glider and learning the parts of the glider in Spanish (Fig. 3-1). Follow the instructions and see if you know what it means to "...use tijeras para cortar a lo largo de la linea trazada."

SIR GEORGE CAYLEY'S GLIDERS

For as long as man has existed on planet earth, he has dreamed of flight. The magic of flight was, for thousands of years, just for gods, angels, and birds.

Early flight did occur in hot-air balloons; however, they were sustained in flight by the buoyancy of a lighter-than-air gas. The balloons did not have much control. Balloons were like clouds. They went where the wind wanted them to go. The secret to true flight was control. This was not discovered until the eighteenth century.

At the beginning of the twentieth century, the most important elements of flight were mastered by Orville and Wilbur Wright: controlled, sustained, and powered.

Englishman George Cayley is given credit for the first design of an aircraft that looks like today's airplanes and gliders. Cayley started experimenting with gliders in 1789, at the age of 23. He had flown several fixed-wing gliders by the year 1809. Cayley made several contributions to the science of flight. He discovered the forces of lift, drag, and thrust. He was the first to use a tail on an aircraft for stability. He observed birds when they were soaring and this gave him the

ACTIVITY: MAKING A GLIDER
ACTIVIDAD: HACIENDO UN PLANEADOR

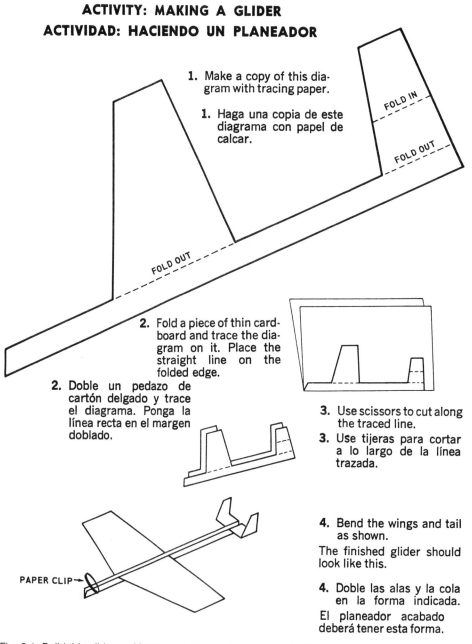

1. Make a copy of this diagram with tracing paper.

1. Haga una copia de este diagrama con papel de calcar.

FOLD IN

FOLD OUT

FOLD OUT

2. Fold a piece of thin cardboard and trace the diagram on it. Place the straight line on the folded edge.

2. Doble un pedazo de cartón delgado y trace el diagrama. Ponga la línea recta en el margen doblado.

3. Use scissors to cut along the traced line.

3. Use tijeras para cortar a lo largo de la línea trazada.

4. Bend the wings and tail as shown.

The finished glider should look like this.

4. Doble las alas y la cola en la forma indicada.

El planeador acabado deberá tener esta forma.

PAPER CLIP →

Fig. 3-1. Build this glider and learn several aeronautical terms in Spanish.

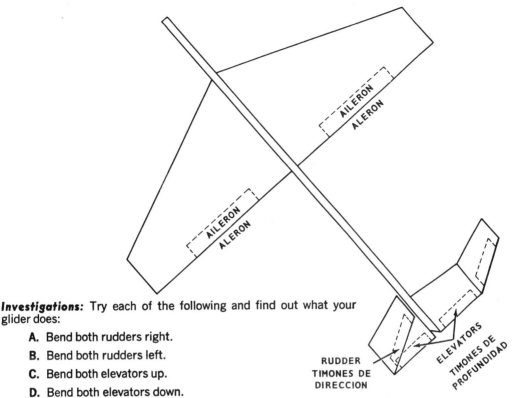

Investigations: Try each of the following and find out what your glider does:

- **A.** Bend both rudders right.
- **B.** Bend both rudders left.
- **C.** Bend both elevators up.
- **D.** Bend both elevators down.
- **E.** Bend the right aileron up and the left aileron down.
- **F.** Bend the right aileron down and the left aileron up.

What conclusions can you draw from the results of these activities?

Investigaciones: Haga las siguientes pruebas y descubra qué es lo que hace su planeador.

- **A.** Doble ambos timones de dirección hacia la derecha.
- **B.** Doble ambos timones de dirección hacia la izquierda.
- **C.** Doble ambos timones de profundidad hacia arriba.
- **D.** Doble ambos timones de profundidad hacia abajo.
- **E.** Doble el alerón derecho hacia arriba y el alerón izquierdo hacia abajo.
- **F.** Doble el alerón derecho para abajo y el alerón izquierdo para arriba.

¿Qué concluye Ud. de los resultados de estas actividades?

Fig. 3-1. Continued.

idea for a fixed-wing glider. He recognized the importance of the curved upper surface of a wing. The curved surface is known as *camber*. Before his death in 1857, George Cayley built a full-size glider with control lines attached that sailed like a kite.

🛑 Building Cayley's 1804 glider

We can re-create a bit of aviation history by making a model of George Cayley's glider. It can be made of styrofoam or balsa wood (Fig. 3-2).

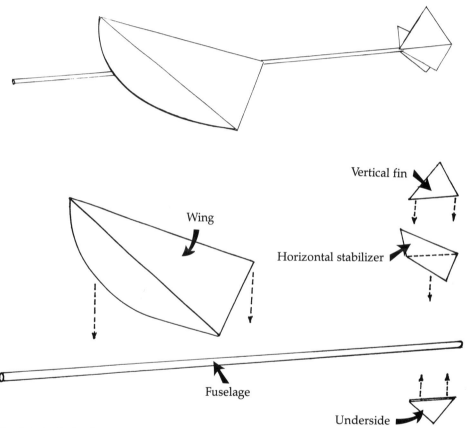

Fig. 3-2. Cayley's glider in 1804 was the first to actually have a shape like a modern airplane.

1. Cut the wings out of a styrofoam food container.
2. Now, cut out the tail pieces.
3. Mount the pieces on a soda straw using a white glue like Elmer's.
4. Put paper clips or clay on the nose for weight.
5. Fly your Cayley glider. If it dives too quickly, remove part of the weight. If it flies steeply upward and stops before going down, add weight.

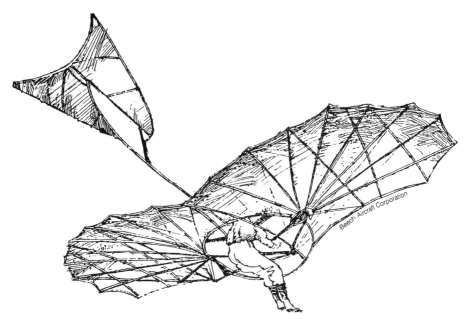

Fig. 3-3. Otto Lilienthal was one of the greatest glider pioneers. He and brother Gustav made numerous glider flights in the years before the Wright brothers flew.

OTTO LILIENTHAL'S GLIDERS

One of the greatest pioneers in the field of gliders was Otto Lilienthal. He and brother Gustav made numerous glider flights in the years before the Wright brothers flew. The hang glider was pioneered by Otto and his technique of shifting weight for control is still used today (Fig. 3-3).

Lilienthal realized that wing-flapping was not the right way to power a flying machine, so he concentrated on learning more about gliders. Lilienthal shared much of what he learned with others, including Orville and Wilbur Wright.

Lilienthal was interested in flying gliders in competition. He dreamed of athletes using gliders in events much like the Olympics. He believed that great strength, coordination, and balance were necessary to fly gliders and the science of flight could be advanced by competition. An interesting kit of Lilienthal's glider is made by the Japanese company DOM. When constructed, it looks somewhat like a strange bird with filmy wings (Fig. 3-4). It is weird, but it will attract more attention from your friends than any other model in your collection. Just tell them it was the world's first hang glider.

Basic assembly requires that you first lay out the die-cut wooden pieces (Fig. 3-5). You can use a good quality wood glue for the subassembly. Testor's wood glue worked fine (Fig. 3-6). If you are familiar with a fast-setting hot glue, that will also do a suitable job. To really make the model look finished, polyester thread was used (Fig. 3-7). This cord gives the model a finished look and, although not a flyer, it is an interesting static model for your collection.

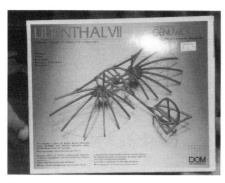

Fig. 3-4. An interesting model kit of Lilienthal's glider is available.

Fig. 3-5. Basic assembly requires laying out the die-cut wooden pieces as shown by student Jason Schierkolk.

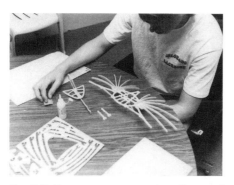

Fig. 3-6. You may use a good quality wood glue for the subassembly. If you are familiar with a fast-setting hot glue, it also does a suitable job.

Fig. 3-7. Polyester thread made the model look finished. The model does not fly, but is an interesting static model for any collection.

If you can't find it at a local hobby shop, write Into The Wind, Boulder, Colorado, which is mentioned in the appendix.

HANG GLIDERS

A modern hang glider is a beautiful sight to see in flight. Hang gliders have been improved in past years and thousands of them take to the skies whenever flying conditions are good.

A hang glider has to be launched from a hill or cliff. The pilot first uses gravity to gain speed. He or she then uses their body weight to cause the glider to turn, bank, dive, and climb (Fig. 3-8).

The hang glider flies like any glider, although the pilot controls it by shifting his or her weight. To roll to the right, the pilot swings to the right while holding the control bar. When the body weight shifts, the glider rolls in that direction. To pitch the nose up or down, the pilot tilts backward or forward by pushing or

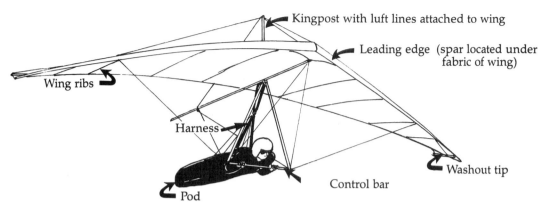

Kingpost with luft lines attached to wing

Leading edge (spar located under fabric of wing)

Wing ribs

Harness

Washout tip

Control bar

Pod

Fig. 3-8. The modern hang glider in flight.

pulling on the control bar. When ready to land, the pilot removes the feet from the pod and gently slows the glider to a walking pace prior to touchdown.

🛑 Flying a toy hang glider

A toy hang glider, the Windseeker, is inexpensive and fun to fly. An address for more information is in the appendix. The pilot is made of heavy-duty plastic and the wing is made of styrofoam. The kit even includes stickers to make the hang glider look authentic. To assemble, simply snap the pilot into the holes in the bottom of the wing and it is ready to fly (Fig. 3-9).

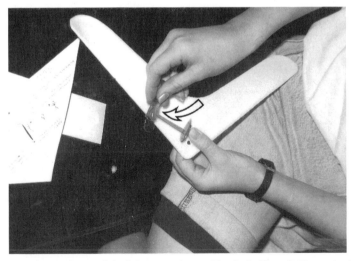

Fig. 3-9. A Windseeker toy hang glider is inexpensive and fun to fly. The pilot is made of heavy-duty plastic and the wing is made of styrofoam. Snap the pilot into the holes in the bottom of the wing and it is ready to fly.

First, a straight-line test flight. Hold the pilot like you would the base of a paper airplane and give it a toss (Fig. 3-10). If the glider turns to one side, gently twist downward on the side that it turned, make another test flight, and repeat the gentle twisting until it flies straight. The glider is capable of doing loops, stalls, and other maneuvers.

Fig. 3-10. Hold the pilot like you would the base of a paper airplane and give it a toss.

If the wing of the Windseeker is ever broken, it can be repaired with a few drops of white glue.

THE FOUR FORCES IN FLIGHT

Four forces act upon any aircraft in flight. The four forces are *lift, thrust, gravity,* and *drag* (Fig. 3-11).

The wings of a glider provide the lift, also known as the *lifting force*. Drag is resistance of the air against the glider's surface.

Lift is the force that keeps the glider flying. Lift works against gravity. When the glider is on the ground, standing still in calm air, only the force of gravity is working on it (Fig. 3-12). When flying, air moving over and under the wings creates the lifting force.

When the glider is moving, the air meeting the wing divides. Part of the air goes over the wing and part of the air goes under the wing. The wing's curvature

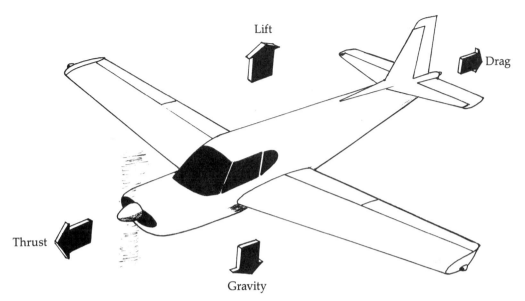

Lift

Drag

Thrust

Gravity

Fig. 3-11. Four forces act upon every aircraft in flight.

Fig. 3-12. When a glider or any aircraft is on the ground, standing still, in calm air, only the force of gravity is affecting it.

makes the air move over the upper surface faster than the air moving underneath the wing. This causes a difference in the pressure of the air. The discovery of this principle unlocked the secret of sustained flight. Daniel Bernoulli, a Swiss scientist, discovered this principle.

Bernoulli's principle states "as the speed of a fluid (such as air) increases, the pressure decreases." This means that the air passing over a wing is moving faster than the air on the underside. The pressure of the faster moving air drops and the wing responds by moving into the lower pressure. This is the lifting force. The pressure on the bottom of the wing is higher. The lower pressure on top of the wing accounts for the greatest percentage of the overall lift. The wing flies because Bernoulli's principle works. (Chapter 5 explains more about wings.)

🛑 Experimenting with Bernoulli's principle

Blowing over the top of a piece of paper in front of your mouth demonstrates Bernoulli's principle. Notice the shape of the curved paper. It would seem that your breath would force the paper down. Just the opposite occurs. Because the air moves faster when it curves up and over the paper, the air pressure drops and the paper moves into the lower pressure (Fig. 3-13). Notice that the curved paper is shaped like the upper surface of a wing (Fig. 3-14), similar to the wing on a Cessna airplane (Fig. 3-15). When air flows over the curved upper surface of this wing, lift is produced, just like the curved paper that Eulah Gibson blew over.

Weight, also known as gravity, is another force acting upon an aircraft. The direction of the weight of the glider always acts downward toward the center of the earth. When an powered airplane tows a sailplane into the air, the airplane provides the forward thrust. Gravity and inertia provide the thrust when the sailplane is flying on its own, moving forward, released from the airplane.

Drag is caused by the surface of the aircraft, such as a glider, when the aircraft disrupts the flow of air around it. Imagine that you were walking waist deep in water. You can feel the drag of the water tugging at you when you try to move. The faster you try to go, the greater the drag. The same holds true for a glider or any other aircraft. The faster the speed, the greater the drag. All of the drag that acts upon a glider is known as *parasite drag*.

Fig. 3-13. When air moves faster as it curves up and over the paper, the pressure drops and the paper moves into the lower pressure.

Fig. 3-14. Notice in this photograph that the curved paper is shaped like the upper surface of a wing.

Fig. 3-15. Compare this wing of a Cessna airplane to the curved paper in Fig. 3-14.

RAILROADER HELPS WRIGHT BROTHERS

Octave Chanute was an aviation pioneer who indirectly helped the Wright brothers with their successful powered flying machine. Chanute was an expert in the field of railroad construction. His knowledge of railroad bridge construction was used in the design of *biplane* wings. Biplane means that the glider or airplane has two wings, one above and one below the main body. Chanute experimented with box kites and found that the basic method of strengthening railroad bridges also gave great strength to his kites. When Chanute started experimenting with gliders, he used the box kite methods to strengthen their wings. The new knowledge that he gained was eagerly shared with others. Some of his principles are used today in aircraft construction.

🛑 Building the box kite

Student Mike Terpinning has constructed a box kite (Fig. 3-16) using a design explained in TAB Books' *Dynamite Kites* (No. 2969) by Jack Wiley and Suzanne Cheatle.

Notice the similarity between the construction of this kite (Fig. 3-17) and one of the Wright Brothers' gliders (Fig. 3-18). Mike's kite was constructed using bridge-building technology and the kite is very light and very strong, ready for a good wind to arise and go flying (Fig. 3-19).

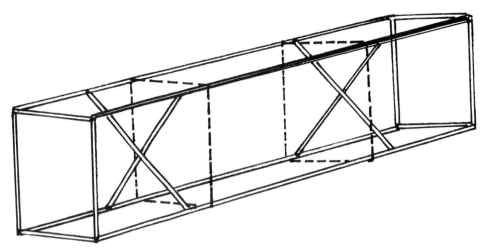

Fig. 3-16. A basic box kite.

Fig. 3-17. Framework of the box kite.

The Wright brothers built gliders before airplanes

The Wright brothers are given credit for being the first to achieve sustained, controlled, and powered flight. Before they were successful with the powered

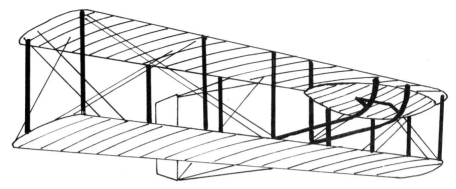

Fig. 3-18. One of the Wright brothers' gliders.

Fig. 3-19. The kite was constructed using bridge building technology for very light weight, yet a strong structure. A good wind is all that is needed to go flying.

airplane, they started experimenting with gliders. One method they used was to fly a glider as if it were a kite. Steady winds helped them experiment with various designs. The Wright brothers were successful with a powered airplane because they were the first to develop a method for control. They believed that power could be added and flight could be sustained only with a fully controllable aircraft; therefore, control had to come first.

🛑 Building the Wright brothers' glider

A simple little glider can be made with styrofoam or balsa wood (Fig. 3-20). You need a styrofoam tray or a $3/32$-inch sheet of balsa wood plank, wooden toothpicks, scissors, and white glue.

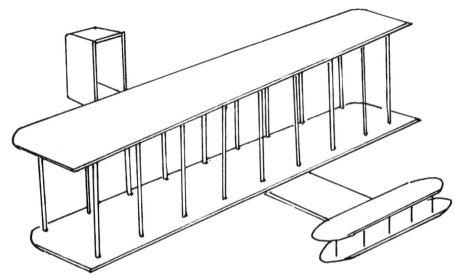

Fig. 3-20. The Wright brothers' glider model will look like this when assembled.

1. Cut out two wings of styrofoam or balsa wood (Fig. 3-21). The wings of the glider are 7 inches from tip to tip (span) and 1 inch from front to rear (chord). The body piece (fuselage) is $4 \times 3/4$ inches. The elevator is $2^1/4 \times 7/16$ inches. One rudder piece is $1^1/4 \times 1/2$ inches and the other rudder piece is $3/4 \times 1/2$ inches.
2. Push toothpicks, lengthwise, through the center of each rudder. Glue each rudder upright at one end of the body; one to the right edge and the other to the left. Next glue on the rudder top.
3. Dip 18 toothpicks in glue and lay the second wing carefully on them using the dots as guides. Press together carefully. Cut a toothpick in half. Glue one piece each to two middle toothpicks to look like propellers. Set all of this aside to dry.
4. Assemble the elevator by dipping five of the one-half toothpick ends in the glue. Place the toothpicks upright on the dots. Dab glue on the tops and place the second elevator on them. Press together carefully.
5. Glue the wings to the center of the body.
6. Glue the elevator to the other end of the body.
7. Tape a dime to the bottom, between the wings and the elevator.
8. Wait for the glue to dry. Examine the glider from left side and compare it

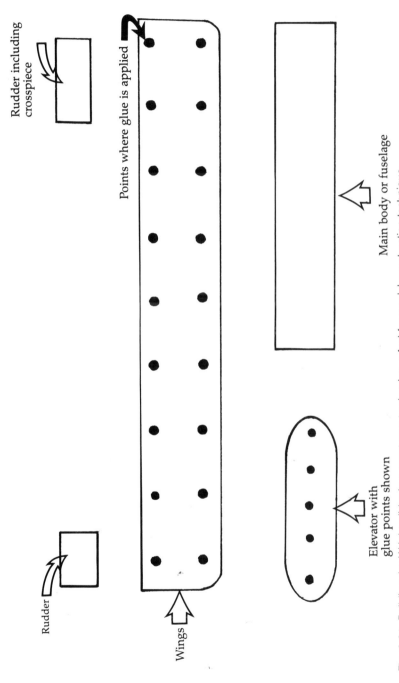

Rudder including crosspiece

Points where glue is applied

Rudder

Wings

Main body or fuselage

Elevator with glue points shown

Fig. 3-21. Building the Wright glider is a great way to develop a feel for model construction technique.

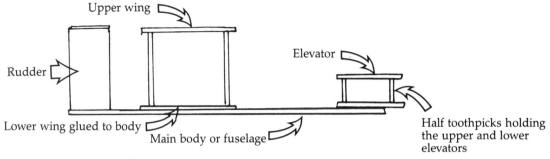

Fig. 3-22. This is how the Wright glider model should look from the side.

to Fig. 3-22. Tape a weight under the nose just below the elevators and it is ready for takeoff.

9. Sail it carefully. Minor adjustments will probably make it a nifty little glider.

SAILPLANES

Gliders, which might be more commonly called sailplanes, of today have the ability to stay aloft for many hours and reach altitude records that were only dreams a few years ago.

When you look at the four forces that act upon an aircraft in flight—thrust, lift, gravity, and drag—you begin to wonder how a glider can achieve so much lift, yet have no power. A glider (Fig. 3-23) has a sleek body (fuselage), no engine, and long thin wings. Maybe it is the long and thin wing that has something to do with it.

Fig. 3-23. A glider has a sleek fuselage, no engine, and long, thin wings.

Scientists who study aircraft and do experiments in aviation technology found that a long and thin wing is extremely efficient. It provides a tremendous amount of lift without creating much drag compared to its lifting ability.

A good glider, also known as a sailplane, will fly a long distance without losing much altitude. The distance is a *glide ratio*. Example: A glide ratio of 20:1 means that a glider at an altitude of one mile (5,280 feet) will glide forward 20 miles before it lands (Fig. 3-24).

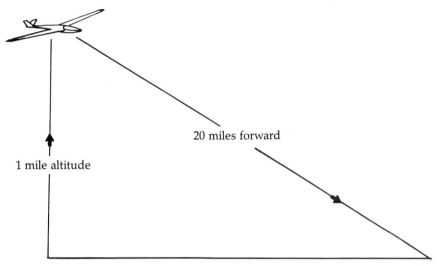

20 miles forward

1 mile altitude

Fig. 3-24. A glide ratio of 20:1 means that a glider one statute mile above the ground (5,280 feet) in altitude will glide forward 20 miles before it lands.

An airplane that is typically flown for training has a glide ratio of approximately 6:1. A high-performance sailplane will have a glide ratio of 30:1. So you see, the secret is in the glider's design. Mainly, in the design of the wing.

Gliders rely on currents of air, known as *thermals*, to keep them aloft. A thermal is like a wind moving upward. When the sun starts heating the earth, the warm air directly above the ground starts to rise. Sailplane pilots look for these thermals. Instruments in the cockpit indicate when a thermal has been found. When the sailplane is in the thermal, a pilot can circle around and around, gaining altitude. You might have noticed a bird sailing around in a thermal on a warm, lazy afternoon. Birds can set their wings like a glider and sail around for long periods of time.

When the pilot has achieved a certain altitude or the thermal is no longer providing enough lift to gain altitude, he or she starts to glide down until another thermal is located. Then the climbing circle, going around and around, starts again. It is like a slide at the park pool or waterpark: go to the top, slide down, then do it over again.

Sailplane pilots can also rely on winds that are blown into mountain ranges and forced upward by the slope of the ground for an area of lift, commonly known as *ridge soaring*.

If a sailplane lands away from the home airport, for instance when attempting to set a distance record—perhaps many hundreds of miles—a chase crew picks it up. The wings are removed and the glider is put into a trailer (Fig. 3-25) to be towed back home. When favorable conditions exist—heating for thermals or winds for ridge soaring—it is time to go flying again.

Fig. 3-25. Sailplane wings are removed at the conclusion of a flight, placed into a trailer with the fuselage, and towed home or to another storage place, ideally an airport.

4

Controlled, sustained, and powered flight

WHILE EXPERIMENTING WITH GLIDERS, the Wright brothers also worked on the problem of finding a suitable engine to power their aircraft. The one that they used was a four-cylinder motor of their own design. The engine produced 12 horsepower and drove two propellers.

The Wright brothers are given credit for being the first to fly because they had control with power. Several other aviation pioneers came very close to achieving flight before the Wright brothers; however, Orville and Wilbur Wright are now recognized because they were able to control their powered aircraft and keep it going under its own power. This meant that the flight was sustained (Fig. 4-1).

Orville remembered the event in *How We Made the First Flight*, which is a publication of the National Air and Space Museum, Smithsonian Institution:

"Monday, December 14th (in the year, 1903), was a beautiful day, but there was not enough wind.... We decided to attempt a flight from the side of the big Kill Devil Hill. We had arranged with the members of the Kill Devil Life Saving Station, which was located a little over a mile from our camp, to inform them when we were ready to make the first trial of the machine. We were soon joined by J.T. Daniels, Robert Wescott, Thomas Beacham, W.S. Dough, and Uncle Benny O'Neal, of the station. We laid the track 150 feet up the hill on a 9 degree slope. With the slope of the track, the thrust of the propellers and the machine starting directly into the wind, we did not anticipate any trouble in getting it up to flying speed.... We did not feel certain the operator could keep the machine balanced on the track.

When the machine had been fastened with a wire to the track, so that it could not start until released by the operator, and the motor had been run to make sure that it was in condition, we tossed a coin to decide who should have

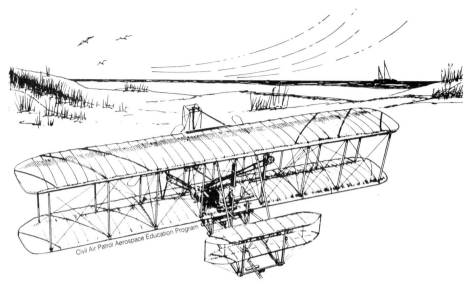

Fig. 4-1. On December 17, 1903, Orville Wright was the first man to achieve controlled, sustained, and powered flight. The first flight achieved a height of 12 feet and the aircraft traveled 120 feet forward.

the first trial. Wilbur won. I took a position at one of the wings, intending to help balance the machine as it ran down the track. But when the restraining wire was slipped, the machine started off so quickly, I could stay with it only a few feet. After a 35 to 40 foot run, it lifted from the rail. But it was allowed to turn up too much. It climbed a few feet, stalled and then settled to the ground near the foot of the hill, 105 feet below. My stop watch showed that it had been in the air just three and one-half seconds. In landing the left wing touched first. The machine swung around, dug the skids into the sand and broke one of them. Several other parts were also broken, but the damage to the machine was not serious....

[The brothers spent the next few days making repairs. On the morning of December 17, they tried again.]

During the night of December 16th, 1903, a strong, cold wind blew from the north. When we arose on the morning of the 17th, the puddles of water, which had been standing about the camp...were covered with ice...we thought it (the wind) would die down before long. When ten o'clock arrived...the wind was as brisk as ever, (so) we decided that we had better get the machine out and attempt a flight.

By the time all was ready, J.T. Daniels, W.S. Dough and A.D. Etheridge, members of the Kill Devil Life Saving Station; W.C. Brinkley of Manteo, and Johnny Moore, a boy from Nags Head, had arrived. Since Wilbur had used his turn in the unsuccessful attempt on the 14th, the right to the first trial now belonged to me. After running the motor a few minutes to heat it up, I released the wire that held the machine to the track and the machine started forward in the wind. Wilbur ran at the side of the machine, holding the wing to balance it on the track. Unlike the start on the 14th, made in calm, the machine, facing a 27 mile wind, started very slowly. Wilbur was able to stay with it till it lifted from the track after the forty-foot run. One of the Life Saving men snapped the camera for us, taking a picture just as the machine had reached the end of the track and had risen to a height of about two feet. The slow forward speed of the machine over the ground is clearly shown in the picture by Wilbur's attitude. He stayed along beside the machine without any effort.

The course of the flight up and down was erratic, partly due to the air, and partly to the lack of experience in handling this machine. The control of the front rudder was difficult on account of its being balanced too near the center. This gave it a tendency to turn itself when started. As a result the machine would rise suddenly to about ten feet, and then suddenly dart for the ground. A sudden dart when a little over a hundred feet from the end of the track, or a little over 120 feet from the point at which it rose into the air, ended the flight. This flight lasted only 12 seconds, but it was nevertheless the first in the history of the world in which a machine carrying a man had raised itself by its own power into the air in full flight and had finally landed at a point as high as that from which it had started."

The Wright's made several more flights that day and the longest was a distance of 852 feet and lasted 59 seconds; Wilbur was at the controls. This longest flight also resulted in minor damage to the elevator supports during a hard landing. Shortly afterward, strong gusty winds damaged the airplane even more and that ended the flight testing.

President Calvin Coolidge signed legislation in 1927 that erected a monument at Kill Devil Hill to honor the Wright's achievement. The 60-foot-tall granite structure carries an inscription:

In commemoration of the conquest of the air by the brothers Wilbur and Orville Wright. Conceived by genius, achieved by dauntless resolution and unconquerable faith.

CONTROL AROUND THREE AXES

Imagine yourself holding a model airplane out in front of you. Okay, hold it straight, as if it were flying away from you. Now, wiggle the wings, or as they commonly say in aviation, *rock* the wings. Study the airplane for a second. Do you see that the airplane is rocking from side to side around the center of the body? A line from the nose to the tail is called the *longitudinal* axis.

Hold the airplane up in front of you again, only this time move the airplane's nose up and down. Notice that the airplane is rocking its nose up and down through a line that goes from side to side, called the *lateral* axis.

Finally, hold the airplane up in front of you and move the nose from side to side. Notice that the tail moves in the opposite direction. The airplane is moving around a line that goes directly through the center, called the *vertical* axis.

These are the three axes (plural) that an airplane moves around (Fig. 4-2): rocking the wings motion, known as *roll*; nose first one way, then the other, known as *yaw*; nose up, nose down motions, known as *pitch*.

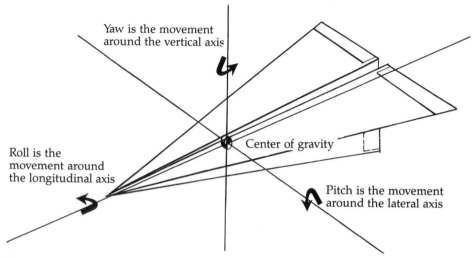

Fig. 4-2. The paper airplane has three axes, just like a real airplane. The arrows show the range of movement around the three axes.

A pilot must be able to control the roll, yaw, and pitch to make an airplane do exactly what he wants while flying.

That was why the Wright brothers were the first. They were able to control the airplane around its three axes. An engine and propellers were used for the power necessary to sustain flight.

An airplane has control surfaces that make it roll, yaw, and pitch. Control surfaces are usually located on the tail section or on the wings. Ailerons (on the wings), the elevator (on the tail's horizontal stabilizer), and the rudder (on the tail's vertical stabilizer) are the control surfaces.

PRIMARY CONTROL SURFACES

All axes of an airplane go through one central point called the *center of gravity*. When one of the control surfaces is moved, the airplane responds by moving around the center of gravity (Fig. 4-2).

Elevator. When the elevator moves up (Fig. 4-3), the tail of the airplane moves down. When the elevator moves down (Fig. 4-4), the tail goes up. Hold your model out in front of you again. Slowly move the tail down. Notice that the nose goes up, which you recall is pitch. Some airplanes have a horizontal stabilizer that does not have a hinged elevator, but pivots near the center; the combined stabilizer and elevator is called a *stabilator* (Fig. 4-5).

Fig. 4-3. When the elevator moves up, the tail of the airplane moves down, the nose goes up, and the airplane starts to climb.

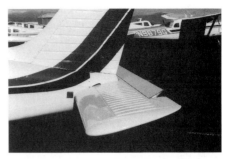

Fig. 4-5. When an airplane does not have an elevator, it probably has a stabilator, which combines the horizontal stabilizer and the elevator in one unit.

Fig. 4-4. When the elevator moves down, the tail of the airplane moves up, the nose goes down, and the airplane starts to descend.

Fig. 4-6. The hinged part of a vertical stabilizer is the rudder. Airplanes made by Mooney Aircraft Corporation have a vertical stabilizer that is not swept, but perpendicular to the ground.

Rudder. When the rudder (Fig. 4-6) is moved to one side, the tail of the airplane moves toward the opposite side, the other way. When the back of the airplane moves one direction, the front of the airplane moves the opposite direction. Recall that nose movement around the vertical axis is yaw.

The rudder in Fig. 4-6 looks unusual because the edge of the vertical stabilizer is perpendicular to the ground, rather than slanted; a slanted stabilizer edge is more common. (Figure 4-6 is the tail section of a Mooney single-engine airplane.)

Ailerons. Roll occurs when one wing rises and the other wing lowers and the airplane enters a *bank*. When the aileron on one wing moves down (Fig. 4-7), the aileron on the opposite wing moves up (Fig. 4-8). Naturally, the opposite occurs when the aileron on the other side moves down. Recall that roll is a movement around the longitudinal axis.

Fig. 4-7. When an aileron is moved down on one wing, the aileron on the opposite wing moves up.

Fig. 4-8. Just the opposite occurs when the aileron on the other side moves down.

🛑 Experimenting with roll, pitch, and yaw

This experiment constructs a paper airplane with control surfaces:

1. Fold the paper in half (Fig. 4-9).
2. Fold back the upper portion (Fig. 4-10). Make sure that the creases are sharp.
3. Fold the paper out flat again and make the next fold as shown by folding the outside edge to the center (Fig. 4-11).
4. The wings are made by carefully folding the upper edge down the bottom line of the fuselage (Fig. 4-12). It is ready to fly.
5. Find the center of gravity (Fig. 4-13) by turning the airplane upside down and balancing the airplane on a finger. Staple the two sides of the fuselage together just ahead of the center of gravity.
6. Make the cuts in the back of the paper airplane using a pair of scissors as shown in Fig. 4-14. (Now that the airplane is finished, the components are easy to identify and are very similar to a real airplane (Fig. 4-15); the noticeable difference is the *elevons*, which are combined elevators and ailerons.)
7. Very carefully bend the elevons, one up and one down. Let's try a roll. Ready? Throw the airplane. Notice how it corkscrews through the air.

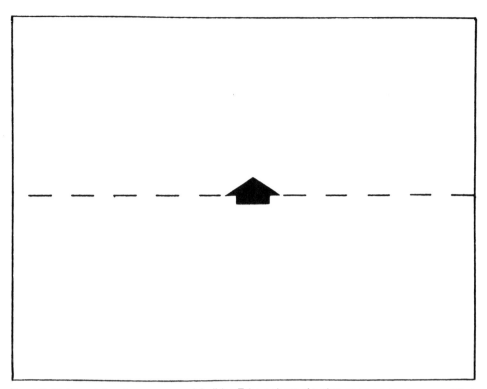

Fig. 4-9. Make a delta wing paper model glider. Take a sheet of typing or computer paper and first fold it in the center.

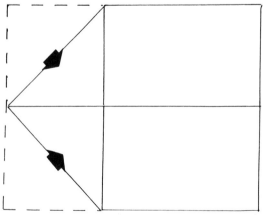

Fig. 4-10. Ends of the paper airplane are folded inward to make a pointed nose. The two end tabs must meet at the center crease.

This is a roll and the airplane is rotating around the longitudinal axis (Fig. 4-15).

8. Next, bend the elevons even with the wing, then bend each elevon up just a little bit, making the bend as even as possible. Ready? Throw it again.

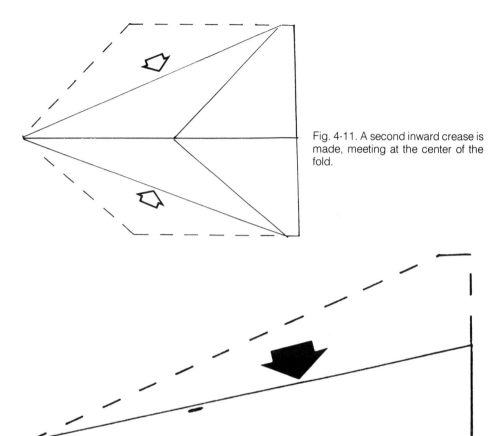

Fig. 4-11. A second inward crease is made, meeting at the center of the fold.

Fig. 4-12. Wings are made by carefully folding the upper edge down the bottom line of the fuselage.

The little airplane will fly away from you and then, almost like magic, its nose will pitch upward. Notice that the airplane does not keep flying up, it eventually drops to the floor, which is known as a *stall*. Any flying aircraft can stall, whether paper model or commercial jetliner. The airflow over the wing is disrupted (made uneven) to the point that the wing is no longer able to create lift, the wing stalls, and the aircraft starts to fall, usually nose first. (If there were a little "paper pilot" inside the model airplane who could magically move the control surfaces just after the stall happens, the airplane might start flying again, known as a *stall recovery*.

9. Bend the elevons even with the wing again. Take the scissors again, and cut a rudder in the back, similar to the elevons. Move the rudder to either side, you get to choose. Ready? Throw the airplane a few times. Notice that the airplane wants to pull its nose to the same side as the fold. Flying to the right or left is a demonstration of yaw.

10. Make the airplane land nice and soft, floating gently downward without darting off in another direction. Make a runway on the floor with masking

Fig. 4-13. Balance the airplane on one finger to find the center of gravity and staple the two sides of the fuselage together just ahead of where the airplane is balanced.

Fig. 4-14. Make cuts in the back of the paper plane as shown, using a pair of scissors.

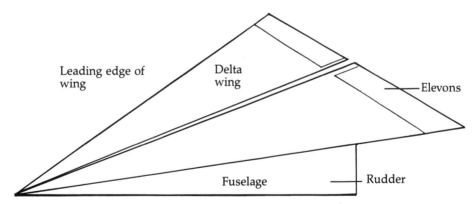

Leading edge of wing

Delta wing

Elevons

Fuselage

Rudder

Fig. 4-15. The paper airplane components are basically the same as any delta wing airplane.

tape or any tape that can be easily removed and not leave sticky material on the floor. (Make a long rectangle, maybe 1 foot wide and 6 feet long, with a strip of tape in the middle to form a *runway centerline*.) Stand back 10 to 15 feet and see if you can make the airplane land on the runway's centerline. You will find that if you put the elevons slightly up, the paper airplane will glide nicely to a soft landing. If the airplane tends to turn to the right, put the left elevon up just a little more. If the airplane goes the opposite direction, adjust the other elevon to straighten the path of flight. If the airplane flies too far, you are throwing it too hard. Practice until the airplane gently floats in for a smooth and straight landing.

A. AILERONS
- AS CONTROL WHEEL IS TURNED LEFT, LEFT AILERON GOES UP, RIGHT AILERON GOES DOWN
- AS CONTROL WHEEL IS TURNED RIGHT, RIGHT AILERON GOES UP, LEFT AILERON GOES DOWN

B. RUDDER
- RIGHT RUDDER PEDAL MOVES RUDDER TO RIGHT
- LEFT RUDDER PEDAL MOVES RUDDER TO LEFT

D. NOSE WHEEL
- RIGHT RUDDER PEDAL TURNS NOSEWHEEL RIGHT
- LEFT RUDDER PEDAL TURNS NOSEWHEEL LEFT

C. ELEVATOR
- FORWARD CONTROL WHEEL MOVEMENT LOWERS ELEVATOR
- REARWARD CONTROL WHEEL MOVEMENT RAISES ELEVATOR

E. BRAKES
- DEPRESSING TOP OF RUDDER PEDAL ACTIVATES THE WHEEL BRAKE
- DEPRESSING BOTH PEDALS ACTIVATES BOTH WHEEL BRAKES

F. FLAPS
- AS FLAP LEVER IS MOVED DOWNWARD WING FLAPS ARE LOWERED

G. POWER CONTROL
- FORWARD MOVEMENT OF THROTTLE INCREASES ENGINE POWER
- REARWARD MOVEMENT OF THROTTLE DECREASES ENGINE POWER

Cessna Aircraft Company, Air Age Education

Fig. 4-16. A pilot must coordinate several controls at once to make an airplane fly. The skills are usually learned in 50 to 100 hours of flying time.

A pilot flying an airplane has the ability to move the control surfaces with hand and foot controls inside the cockpit (Fig. 4-16). Learning about an airplane and all its parts might seem like learning a new language, but this is still English, simply the language of aviation.

THE AIRPLANE AND ITS PARTS

Practically every part of an airplane (Fig. 4-17) is designed for flight or flight support. The fuselage (#9) supports the wings and tail surfaces. The cockpit is where

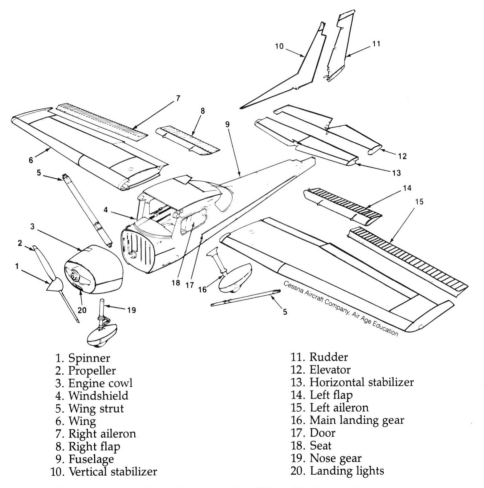

1. Spinner	11. Rudder
2. Propeller	12. Elevator
3. Engine cowl	13. Horizontal stabilizer
4. Windshield	14. Left flap
5. Wing strut	15. Left aileron
6. Wing	16. Main landing gear
7. Right aileron	17. Door
8. Right flap	18. Seat
9. Fuselage	19. Nose gear
10. Vertical stabilizer	20. Landing lights

Fig. 4-17. Every part of an airplane is designed for flight or flight support.

the pilot sits and controls the aircraft. The engine is attached to the fuselage and is located under the cowling (#3). The propeller (#2) is attached to the engine and provides forward thrust for flight. The spinner (#1) channels the airflow into the engine. The landing gear (#19 and #16) support the aircraft while on the ground.

The ailerons (#7 and #15) make the airplane's wings bank up or down for turns around the longitudinal axis (roll). The vertical stabilizer (#10) supports the rudder (#11), which turns the airplane around the vertical axis (yaw). The horizontal stabilizer (#13) supports the elevator (#12), which makes the airplane's nose go up or down around the vertical axis (pitch). The flaps (#8 and #14) allow the airplane to descend during a landing at a steeper angle without gaining unwanted speed. (The flaps also provide more lift by increasing the camber of the upper wing surface.) The wings (#6) provide the lift that allows the aircraft to fly.

The cockpit has many instruments that give the pilot vital data about the flight. Basic instruments are found in any flight training airplane (Fig. 4-18).

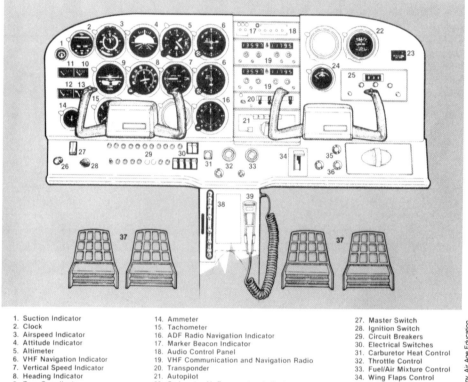

1. Suction Indicator	14. Ammeter	27. Master Switch
2. Clock	15. Tachometer	28. Ignition Switch
3. Airspeed Indicator	16. ADF Radio Navigation Indicator	29. Circuit Breakers
4. Attitude Indicator	17. Marker Beacon Indicator	30. Electrical Switches
5. Altimeter	18. Audio Control Panel	31. Carburetor Heat Control
6. VHF Navigation Indicator	19. VHF Communication and Navigation Radio	32. Throttle Control
7. Vertical Speed Indicator	20. Transponder	33. Fuel/Air Mixture Control
8. Heading Indicator	21. Autopilot	34. Wing Flaps Control
9. Turn Coordinator	22. Carburetor Air Temperature Indicator	35. Cabin Heat Control
10. Fuel Gauge (Right Tank)	23. Flight Hour Indicator	36. Cabin Air Control
11. Fuel Gauge (Left Tank)	24. Exhaust Gas Temperature Gauge	37. Rudder/Brake Pedals
12. Oil Temperature Gauge	25. ADF Radio	38. Elevator Trim Control
13. Oil Pressure Gauge	26. Engine Primer	39. Microphone

Fig. 4-18. Many instruments and special radios help the pilot fly the airplane safely.

Parts of the airplane in Fig. 4-17 can be located on a real airplane, such as a Cessna Skylane (Fig. 4-19). Give it a try.... Some airplanes have wings mounted at the top of the fuselage and other airplanes have the wings mounted near the bottom. A Beechcraft Bonanza (Fig. 4-20) has its wings mounted at the bottom.

Fig. 4-19. This Cessna Skylane is similar to but larger than the Cessna 152 in the illustration of parts. Recognize the parts?

Fig. 4-20. Aerodynamic drag is reduced by this V-shaped tail, which is commonly called a ruddervator.

The parts and components are about the same as the Cessna; however, the Bonanza has a strange looking tail. The vertical stabilizer and horizontal stabilizer are combined on the Bonanza into a V tail, called a *ruddervator*, which partially reduces aerodynamic drag. High performance sailplanes might use this very efficient V-tail (Fig. 4-21).

Fig. 4-21. Certain high performance sailplanes use this type of tail, which is very efficient.

THAT WONDERFUL WING

An airplane is a thing of beauty in flight. It looks graceful. It looks like it is supposed to be up there flying. A bird in flight reveals the motions of its marvelously lightweight feathery wings (Fig. 4-22). An airplane in flight relies on its wings. Wings are made for flying. A pilot who has learned the art of flying and is officially certificated by the Federal Aviation Administration, has earned his "wings." (Commonly, when a student has flown an airplane alone—*solo*—the student may then be called a pilot.)

Scientists have a name for a wing: *airfoil*. An airfoil is any surface that provides a lifting (aerodynamic) force when a flow of air passes around it. The parts of an airfoil (Fig. 4-23) are *leading edge*; *upper* and *lower camber*; *trailing edge*; and

Fig. 4-22. A bird in flight is a wonderful display of nature's wings.

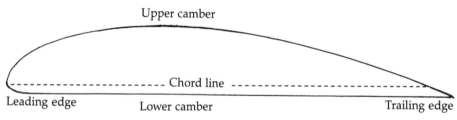

Upper camber

------ Chord line ------

Leading edge   Lower camber   Trailing edge

Fig. 4-23. Components of an airfoil.

chord. (Recall that the air moving over and under a wing is the relative wind.) Can you name the parts of a real airplane's wings? (Fig. 4-24)

When an airplane is ready for takeoff, the pilot adds power to make the engine run faster and turn the prop faster. This causes the airplane to move forward. The air starts to flow over, around, and under the airplane. This air (rela-

Fig. 4-24. Can you name the parts of this wing?

tive wind) is moving in the opposite direction. Remember that when the relative wind moves over the top of the wing, the air has to flow past faster than it does flowing underneath the wing. Also remember that, according to Bernoulli law, this faster flowing air has lower pressure. When the pressure drops, the wing rises upward into the lower pressure area. This is the force of lift. If there is enough lifting force, the whole airplane shall rise and move away from the earth, opposing gravity.

There are several ways of producing more lift (Fig. 4-25):

- Increasing the speed of the air flowing around it.
- Increasing the curvature of the top of the wing.
- Tilting the wing slightly upward toward the relative wind, commonly known as increasing the *angle of attack*.
- Enlarging the wing for more wing surface area.

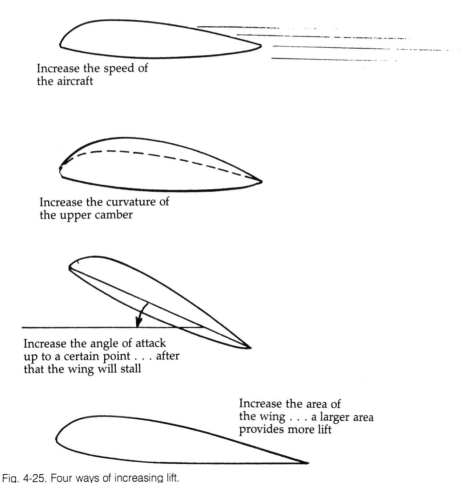

Increase the speed of
the aircraft

Increase the curvature of
the upper camber

Increase the angle of attack
up to a certain point . . . after
that the wing will stall

Increase the area of
the wing . . . a larger area
provides more lift

Fig. 4-25. Four ways of increasing lift.

An airliner's takeoff demonstrates the four ways of producing more lift from a wing. The pilot lowers the leading and trailing edge flaps to increase the camber (increasing the curvature). These flaps also increase the wing area (enlarging the surface). As the airliner rolls out onto the runway, the captain announces: "Flight attendants, prepare for takeoff," and after that announcement the captain adds power and the airliner starts to move faster and faster down the runway (increasing the air's speed flowing over the wing). As the airliner rolls down the runway, faster and faster, it reaches a point where the captain pulls the nose up (increasing the angle of attack).

As the airliner flies higher and faster, the flaps are retracted. The pilot doesn't need them any longer because the speed of the airplane is providing most of the lift. The captain lowers the nose at a prescribed altitude, which reduces the angle of attack and the airliner now flies straight and level.

🛑PROPELLER—A WING THAT IS LIFTING FORWARD

A propeller is a wing that goes around and around extremely fast. The four ways of increasing lift come into play when the engine turns the propeller. Take a close look at the propeller.

Near the center of the propeller, commonly called the *hub* (Fig. 4-26), rotation speed is relatively slower than at the tip. This means that a large camber and high angle of attack are necessary to produce a proper amount of forward lift. Outward from the center (Fig. 4-27), the propeller is moving faster and a shallower angle of attack is necessary to produce a proper amount of forward lift. The area of the propeller is increased at this point to balance thrust (lift). The propeller's tip (Fig. 4-28) has a smaller area, shallower angle of attack, and less camber because the propeller's speed is so high. A propeller might be severely damaged if the engine's speed is excessive and causes the propeller tip to exceed the speed of sound.

Fig. 4-26. A propeller is turning slower at the center compared to the tips.

Fig. 4-27. Outward from the center, the faster moving propeller does not need as much angle of attack.

Fig. 4-28. The area, angle of attack, and camber are reduced at the propeller tips because the speed is so high.

Building and flying the Silver Star Sleeper

David DeLapp, a science teacher at George Washington High School, Denver, makes and flies rubber band-powered free flight model airplanes. One aircraft, which he calls the *Silver Star Sleeper*, has been so successful over the years, that DeLapp is selling a kit.

The kit features a complete set of illustrated directions. A completed aircraft flies for 25 seconds to more than a minute, compared to 10 or 15 seconds for other similar aircraft.

The kit (Fig. 4-29) was designed for teachers and students by a teacher who has been in education for 24 years. The kit allows for easy storage. It is made of inexpensive materials, and allows the builder infinite variety of design. The *Sleeper* has 12 pages of fully illustrated directions. It is made of top-grade balsa wood, Japanese tissue paper, and the highest quality rubber band for a motor. Additional performance supplies (Fig. 4-30) include a winder to quickly wind up the rubber band and rubber lubricant to give even more power.

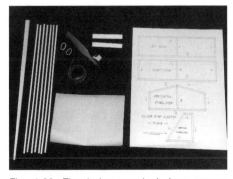

Fig. 4-29. The balsa wood airplane comes with 12 pages of fully illustrated directions.

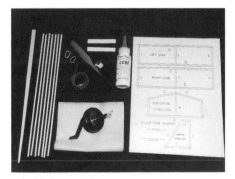

Fig. 4-30. Additional performance supplies include a winder to quickly wind up the rubber band and a lubricant to give even more power.

Fig. 4-31. Storage is in a large shoe box or small shipping box.

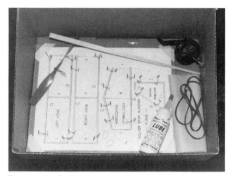

Fig. 4-32. Builders can also store extra parts, winders, glue, spare rubber bands, and the like, in the box.

Storage might be a large shoe box or small shipping box (Fig. 4-31). The plane may be disassembled after each flight and stored in a homemade hangar. A builder may store extra parts, winders, glue, spare rubber bands, and the like, in the box (Fig. 4-32).

The airplane was designed to be compact in size. The plans are on $8^{1}/_{2}$-×-11-inch paper that can be easily copied.

Follow the instructions to build the airplane (Fig. 4-33). Supplies are common household items (Fig. 4-34): ordinary paper-cutting scissors, sandpaper or an emery board, glue, cardboard, waxed paper, and straight pins.

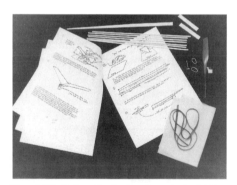

Fig. 4-33. Follow the instructions to build the balsa airplane.

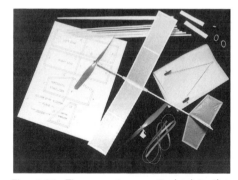

Fig. 4-34. These parts are attached to the fuselage.

Wings and tail surfaces are built according to the instructions, then attached to the fuselage to become a flying model airplane (Fig. 4-35). An optional landing gear with wheels is available to make a traditional takeoff roll. Note that the wing is attached to the fuselage with rubber bands, which permits moving the wing forward or backward to dramatically alter flight capabilities.

Hold onto the airplane (with your hand clear of the propeller) or anchor it solidly, wind up the propeller, release the propeller, and look at all of that power

Fig. 4-35. The completed airplane is ready to go.

Fig. 4-36. Wind up the propeller, let it go, and look at all that power.

(Fig. 4-36). Experienced builders can modify the airplane to fly much longer. The airplane is designed to be extremely stable and will easily fly on windy days.

Make 300 rubber band winds without lube or 960 winds with lube. Average time in the air is about 34 seconds and the record is nine minutes. An address to obtain information from Silver Star Systems is in the appendix.

🛑 The Ryan STA

This remarkable little $25 styrofoam airplane can outperform models that cost more than $100. An MRC Tamiya Ryan STA may be built to suit practically any preference: simple glider; rubber band-power; or a small-engine power for radio controlled flight. The airplane may be painted in bright colors in a personal design, or duplicate one of the paint schemes used on the actual aircraft (Fig. 4-37). The actual Ryan STA was perhaps one of the most beautiful airplanes of all time; this model looks like the real one and flies like a dream.

Fig. 4-37. Dawn Ragain takes a look at the Ryan STA model box to get some styling ideas.

Building and flying the Ryan STA

One of the first steps in building any model is to read the instructions thoroughly (Fig. 4-38). When building a flying model, it is important that the wing

Fig. 4-38. Thoroughly read the instructions of every model project immediately after the box is opened.

Fig. 4-39. Dawn is using a carpenter's square to make sure the vertical stabilizer is perpendicular with the fuselage and the horizontal stabilizer.

and tail surfaces are perfectly aligned. Dawn Ragain is using a carpenter's square (Fig. 4-39) to make sure the vertical stabilizer is perpendicular to the fuselage and the horizontal stabilizer.

Next comes the *powerplant,* which is a more common aeronautical term for an aircraft engine. (The FAA certificates a person who works on airplanes as an *air-*

Fig. 4-40. The Ryan STA's rubber band engine should be checked when the airplane is fully assembled, before any painting.

Fig. 4-41. Spray a mist coat first and let it get tacky before spraying the next coat.

frame and powerplant mechanic, which is typically abbreviated A&P.) We are going to build this airplane with rubber band power. The instruction sheet explains how to hook up the powerful rubber band to the propeller. One of the nicest features of this kit is the *gear reduction* system that allows longer flights and better rates of climb. Check the powerplant and gear reduction system (Fig. 4-40).

Paint the airplane if you like, but remember that paint is additional weight and additional weight cuts down on performance. A plain white styrofoam model is boring, so let's give it some color.

The first step is to pick a paint scheme. Dawn selected the scheme on the model's box. The airplane is first painted white using Testor's enamel. Ask your local hobby shop owner for the right kind of enamel that won't damage or melt styrofoam. Dawn used Testor's model master custom enamel classic white and it did not affect the styrofoam. Follow the instructions on the can. Shake the can before using. A initial mist coat (Fig. 4-41) should get tacky before shooting the remaining coats. It is better to spray lightly several times for a smooth finish, rather than spray heavily and risk bubbles and runs.

Paint must be completely dry (ideally, 24 hours or more) before taping the surface for stripes. Dawn is using plastic tape. If you really want to do an outstanding job, go to a local automotive paint supply store and ask for a roll of #471 tape. When you stripe off the model (Fig. 4-42), your finished paint lines will be crisp and professional looking. This tape is great for making a model look right.

Parts of the model that are not supposed to be red should be completely masked (Fig. 4-43) with paper and regular masking tape. Dawn elected to make the second color Testor's spray enamel gloss red. When the second color is completely dry, the tape should be carefully removed, and the rest of the airplane finished with tape stripes as desired.

Fig. 4-42. Plastic adhesive tape is great for making a model look right.

Fig. 4-43. Dawn went all out to make this a gorgeous model.

HELICOPTERS

Helicopters are complicated flying machines that fall under the category of *rotorcraft* (Fig. 4-44). They may be considered complicated because helicopters have

Fig. 4-44. Helicopters are complicated flying machines, also known as rotorcraft. They have the amazing ability to take off vertically, fly backward, sideways, or just hover in the air.

the amazing ability to take off vertically, fly backward, sideways, or just hover in the air.

The controls of a helicopter are different than an airplane. The cockpit has what looks like the standard control stick directly in front of the pilot (Fig. 4-45), this stick is called the *cyclic*. Beside the pilot's seat is another stick (Fig. 4- 46), called the *collective*. The *throttle* is at the end of the collective (Fig. 4-47). Two pedals are on the floor (Fig. 4-48).

Pitch and roll are controlled by the cyclic. Vertical movement is controlled by

Fig. 4-45. One of two control sticks in a helicopter is the cyclic.

Fig. 4-46. The other of two control sticks is the collective, which is beside the pilot's seat.

Fig. 4-47. The engine throttle is at the end of the collective control.

Fig. 4-48. Two pedals on the floor help the helicopter make turns.

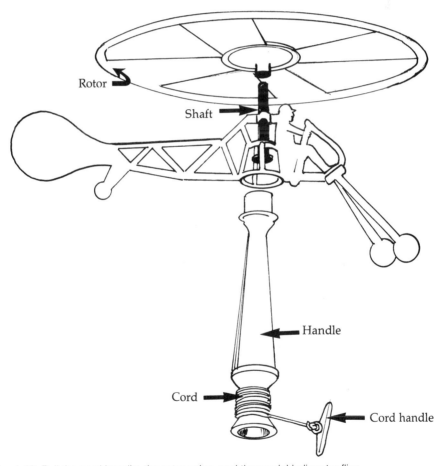

Fig. 4-49. Pull the cord handle, the rotor spins, and the model helicopter flies.

Fig. 4-50. Check the area around you for safety clearances and pull the cord.

Fig. 4-51. Watch the helicopter after it takes off and warn anyone who might come too close to it.

the collective; engine (powerplant) is controlled by the throttle. Yaw is controlled with the pedals.

When the pilot adds power with the throttle and lifts up on the collective, the helicopter rises from the ground. After clearing the ground sufficiently, the pilot moves the cyclic forward and the helicopter pitches its nose down, which provides *forward lift* and the aircraft moves ahead.

A helicopter is like any other aircraft, capable of roll, pitch, and yaw, controlled by movements of the main *rotor blades* and *tail rotor*.

🛑 Experimenting with a model helicopter

Model helicopters are difficult to build and make fly. However, there is a toy (Fig. 4-49), the Hi-Flight helicopter that does reasonably well. (The appendix has the address to obtain the Hi-Flight helicopter.)

The instructions card provides a glimpse into the model:

1. Remove unassembled helicopter from display card.
2. Trim wheels, shaft, and cord handle from rotor.
3. Insert shaft through body.
4. Press rotor over end of shaft.
5. Slide wheels over front end of body.
6. Tie end of cord to cord handle.
7. Wind the cord around the spool end of the handle.
8. Set the helicopter on the conical end of the handle.
9. Hold the handle straight in either hand and pull the cord.

Cautions: Do not pull too hard on the cord because the rotorblade or shaft might break (Fig. 4-50). The spinning rotorblades are dangerous. Do not point the model at someone. Make sure that the area immediately around you is clear (Fig. 4-51) and that anybody close by is watching the model, prepared to avoid it, if it flies too close.

5

Flight profiles and airports

WHEN AN AIRPLANE FLIES FROM ONE POINT TO ANOTHER, it follows a *flight profile*. This means that it follows basically the same pattern every time. The first phase of a flight profile is takeoff. The pilot of an airplane moves the airplane from the parking spot, across the ramp past other parked airplanes, down a lane of pavement, and eventually onto the runway. *Taxi* is the term used to describe driving an airplane while it is on the ground.

The pilot stops the airplane before moving onto the runway and does an engine *runup* to make sure that all flight systems are OK before takeoff. The pilot then moves the airplane onto the active runway, applies power, and the airplane starts the takeoff roll. When the airplane reaches a certain speed, the pilot pulls back on the control wheel or stick, the nose rises slightly, then the airplane rises completely off the ground and is flying.

Climb is the second phase of the flight, maintaining a prescribed angle of climb and a prescribed climb airspeed. The climb continues until the airplane reaches a desired altitude.

The next phase of the flight profile is cruise and it might be short or long. A short flight might be near the airport to practice flying skills. A long flight might be away from the airport, landing at another airport, known as a *cross-country* flight (Fig. 5-1).

Descent phase is meant to lose altitude and prepare for a landing approach.

The last phase of the flight profile is the landing approach. Whether approaching in clouds or in clear skies, a pilot flies the airplane through a series of maneuvers that makes the airplane line up with the runway, normally pointed into any wind for better control and a shorter landing distance.

Taxi after landing, from the runway to the parking spot, is simply backtracking through the pre-takeoff taxi steps.

AIRPORT LAYOUT

The part of the United States government that controls aviation is the Federal Aviation Administration. The FAA, as it is more commonly known, has certain

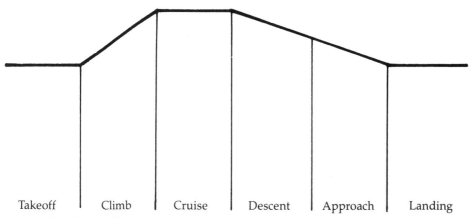

| Takeoff | Climb | Cruise | Descent | Approach | Landing |

Fig. 5-1. The flight profile.

identification standards for airport layout that help a pilot know where to taxi, take off, and land: lighting colors, runway numbers, painted stripes, and signs. Most of the identification standards are different than highway and street signs for cars.

Runways are laid out according to the numbers of a compass. A compass has 360 degrees. Starting at north, or zero, a compass is numbered from 0–360 moving clockwise around a circle (Fig. 5-2). If you stand up and point to the north, you will pointing to compass heading of zero. Turn right and point to the east—you have just turned 90 degrees and the compass heading is the same, 90 degrees. Continue turning right and point to the south—180 degrees. Turn again to the right to the west— 270 degrees. One more turn to the right to face north again—360 degrees, which is also 0 degrees.

Perhaps the compass demonstration helps you visualize a common statement made in everyday life, not just in aviation: "I started the project and halfway through it I made a 180-degree turn and forgot about it." The person turned away from the project and abandoned it.

Repeat the same pointing procedure, but this time move to the right 10 degrees at a time to divide the distance between north and east into nine equal turns:

Start at zero:
10
20
30
40
50
60
70
80
90

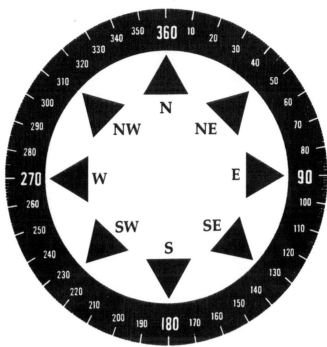

Fig. 5-2. Starting at north, or zero, a compass is numbered from 0 through 360 moving around clockwise.

Now, rather than saying 10, 20, 30, and the like, drop the zero and, pointing the same directions, say,

Start at zero:
"Runway 1,"
"Runway 2,"
"Runway 3,"
"Runway 4,"
and so on.

That is a basic understanding of how airport runways get laid out. Runway 1 is actually very close to a compass heading of 10 degrees; Runway 2 is actually close to a heading of 20 degrees, and so on. If you are standing on Runway 18, you're looking south, or 180 degrees.

(Sometimes the precise heading along the center of the runway is different than the runway number, for instance, Runway 17 might have a precise heading of 168 degrees; the FAA rounds off the runway's number to 17 for simplicity.)

🛑 Recognizing a runway's direction

(Each step of the safety checklist might not be required; nevertheless, verify any steps that do apply.) Armed with the knowledge that one or two digits identify the takeoff or landing direction of an airplane off or onto a runway, you should be able to identify the correct direction based upon the compass divisions and the number:

- Runway 27? That represents a heading of 270 degrees, pointing toward the west. (Correct answers to the following runways are at the end of this chapter.)
- Runway 31?
- Runway 5?
- Runway 24?
- Runway 4?
- Runway 36?

Airport lighting

Runways and taxiways have different colored lights (Fig. 5-3). Many blue lights are visible at an airport at night. The blue lights direct the pilot along the

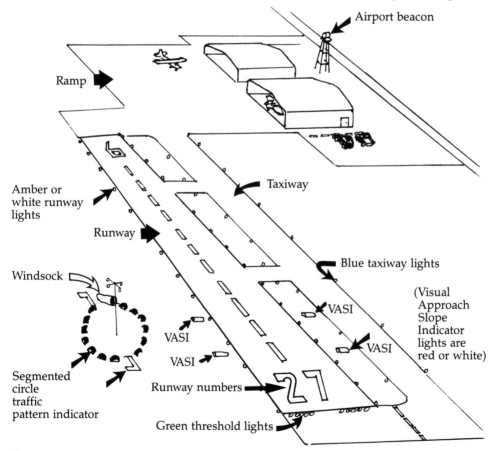

Fig. 5-3. A beacon that flashes white and yellow is at a seaplane base for water landings.

taxiways. Runways will usually have white or yellow lights around them. The beginning of a runway will have a row of green lights facing the pilot during the landing approach. Red lights outline unsafe areas and an airplane is not supposed to be in those areas.

The *rotating beacon* lights help pilots identify an airport at night, when other lights, such as freeway lights, might be mistaken for runway lights. Some beacons flash green and white colors, which mean that it is a civilian airport, open to anyone. If a beacon flashes green and two whites, it is a military airport, open only to military airplanes, except when the pilot of any airplane has an emergency and needs to land immediately for safety reasons. If a beacon flashes yellow and white, it is a seaplane airport where airplanes can land on the water.

A large airport might have an *air traffic control tower* (Fig. 5-4) where women and men direct airplanes and helicopters if they are taxiing on ground, taking off, landing, or even flying overhead, without landing at that airport. The controllers keep aircraft apart, but the pilots share the responsibility and also keep a sharp eye out for other aircraft.

Fig. 5-4. A large airport might have a tower where air traffic controllers manage the movement of aircraft on the ground and in the air.

An airplane service business is a *fixed-base operator*, for short, called an FBO. Often there will be airplane sales, repair services, and a flight training school located at the FBO.

THE TOTAL AIR TRANSPORTATION SYSTEM

Cessna Aircraft Company has granted permission to use excerpts from its Air Age Education program to help understand how the air transportation system works, starting with a look at the overall picture of airports and air travel (Fig. 5-5).

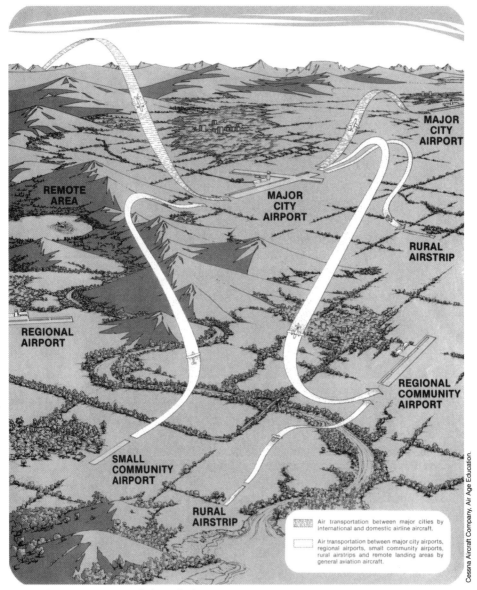

Fig. 5-5. Airports are extremely important.

Flying is the primary means of travel between large cities in this country. Airliners are well suited to moving large numbers of people over great distances. Smaller general aviation aircraft are also well suited to moving people between cities. Even the smallest community can have access to the air transportation network.

Major city airports are usually served by international (foreign countries) and domestic (inside the United States) airline flights. Commuter airliners carry passengers and cargo from smaller regional airports to major city airports. Air taxi flights also carry passengers and cargo from airport to airport. The smaller, personal, general aviation aircraft can provide flight for even the smallest communities with an airport to larger city airports.

General aviation airplanes play a major role in helping people get from place to place. Even remote areas where no airports exist can be reached by temporary landing strips. Many float-equipped airplanes can take off from rivers and lakes and land at a regular airport because wheels are attached to the floats.

A small community airport (Fig. 5-6) supports general aviation flying. A Cessna 402 is shown in Fig. 5-6 as a typical commuter that flies passengers and cargo between major city airports and smaller community airports. A Cessna Citation II in Fig. 5-6 represents a small jet that might be owned by a company in a large city doing business in the smaller community.

Community airports will often have facilities for training student pilots. Air taxi service (hiring an airplane and pilot to fly you someplace) and air ambulances are available when needed. Agricultural aircraft are parked in the upper portion of Fig. 5-6. Many small communities are agricultural centers and the airplane plays a major role in crop production.

Large airliners are seen at a major city airport (Fig. 5-7). This service connects airports around the world and across the United States. Also note that the major city airport (Fig. 5-7) has an air taxi, an air ambulance, training airplanes, and commuter aircraft. All are part of the system that brings regional and rural air traffic into the total air transportation system.

(STOP) Landing simulations

Several years back there was a super game called U-Fly-It. I bought one of these for my children at Christmas and spent most of the holiday playing with it myself. It consisted of a tough little plastic model airplane equipped with eye hooks on top of the fuselage. The kit had a runway to lay out on the floor. One end of a nylon cord was attached at some higher point across the room and the other end of the cord was attached to a control stick. The toy is no longer available, but with a few simple materials and a little time, you can assemble everything yourself and start the landing fun.

1. Buy a cheap toy airplane (Fig. 5-8) and put two eye hooks on top of the fuselage (Fig. 5-9).
2. Use self-tapping eye hooks that do not require drilling holes (Fig. 5-10).

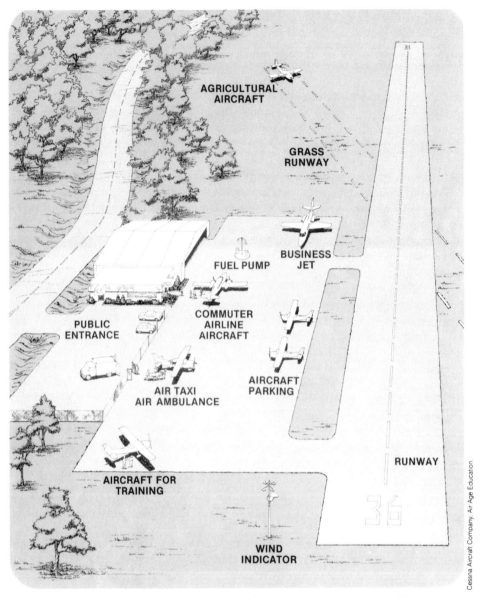

AGRICULTURAL
AIRCRAFT

GRASS
RUNWAY

FUEL PUMP

BUSINESS
JET

PUBLIC
ENTRANCE

COMMUTER
AIRLINE
AIRCRAFT

AIRCRAFT
PARKING

AIR TAXI
AIR AMBULANCE

RUNWAY

AIRCRAFT FOR
TRAINING

WIND
INDICATOR

Fig. 5-6. A small community airport can stay busy with general aviation aircraft activity.

3. Lay out a runway on the floor using masking tape or any tape that does not leave a sticky spot when you pull it up (Fig. 5-11).
4. Get a spool of nylon fishing line and tie one end at some high place (Fig. 5-12), like a pipe in a basement. (Find someone to help you; use a stable ladder to climb upon.)
5. Unroll the fishing line toward the runway and stop at the opposite end of the runway. You and the other person should "eye ball" the fishing line to

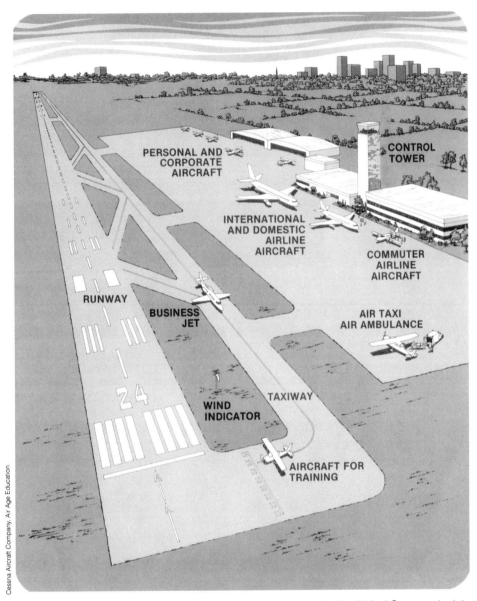

Fig. 5-7. A large, major city airport can handle airlines that fly within the United States and might handle airlines that fly to and from foreign countries.

make sure that it runs straight down the runway. Move the high end of the fishing line, if necessary, to make it line up with the runway. As a last resort, move the runway to make it line up with the fishing line.

6. Securely fasten the fishing line to a stick, perhaps a sawn off wooden broom handle, as shown in the figures. (Ask your parents for an old worn out broom before cutting off the handle of a new broom. Get help from an adult to saw off the handle.)

Fig. 5-8. Buy an inexpensive plastic toy airplane.

Fig. 5-9. Put two eye hooks on top of the fuselage.

Fig. 5-10. The eye hook holes should face the front of the airplane.

Fig. 5-11. Lay out a runway on the floor with masking tape or another tape that can be removed without leaving adhesive on the floor.

7. The helper should hang the airplane on the high end of the nylon fishing line and hold the airplane (Fig. 5-13).

8. You sit down at the opposite end of the runway, looking straight down the runway centerline at the airplane that the helper is holding.

9. Put one end of the stick on the floor, again at the centerline of the runway. This would be a good time to adjust tension on the fishing line with

Fig. 5-12. Get a spool of nylon fishing line and tie one end at a high place, like a pipe in the basement.

Fig. 5-13. A helper slips the eye hooks over the fishing line. Perhaps the helper could be called a copilot.

enough slack to make sure that the airplane can land on the floor without sliding to the stick. Additional fishing line tension adjustments might be necessary during test flights.

10. On your command, the helper releases the little airplane. The airplane starts its approach and flies down the cord toward you.

11. You have to fly it with the stick and make it land on the runway (Fig. 5-14), hopefully on the centerline. By the time the airplane arrives, it is flying fast and you have to make it land properly without crashing.

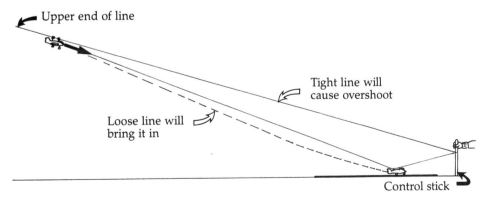

Upper end of line

Tight line will cause overshoot

Loose line will bring it in

Control stick

Fig. 5-14. Fly the toy airplane with the stick and make the airplane land on the runway.

12. Let the helper fly and you release the airplane. It is easy to set up and can give two or more people hours of fun. You may use many different airplanes. Dawn Ragain has flown an F-15 Eagle (Fig. 5-15) and a pontoon-equipped seaplane (Fig. 5-16). A variation on this theme is trying to make a seaplane land in a swimming pool. Use your imagination to demonstrate different flying skills and different airports...safely.

Fig. 5-15. Dawn Ragain lands an F-15 Eagle.

Fig. 5-16. A floatplane model was tested on the carpet, hoping for a hot summer day to play the game in a pool and simulate landing on a lake.

Here are the runway heading answers:

- Runway 31: 310 degrees, northwest;
- Runway 5: 50 degrees, northeast;
- Runway 24: 240 degrees, southwest;
- Runway 4: 40 degrees, north northeast; and
- Runway 36: 360 degrees, north.

6

Space and spacecraft

WHAT IS SPACE?
What is it like there?
What if you could go out there and see for yourself?
What would you find?
Let's explore it...

You already know that the whole universe is made up of *matter* and *energy*. Matter is atoms and molecules. Energy is a force. The force of energy makes matter do things.

Normally, atoms are very close together. In space, however, atoms are far apart. So you ask, what is in between the atoms? Space. Space is a place where atoms are far apart and about the only thing in between the atoms is energy.

When there is nothing in a large area, you might say that the area is a vacuum. Space is not a perfect vacuum. A few atoms or molecules are always floating around. For there to be a perfect vacuum, there would have to be perfectly nothing.

Also out in space, the temperature is extremely low. Sometimes the temperature can approach what is known as *absolute zero*, −459.67 °F.

Although we cannot see energy, it is there. In space, there are streams of energy going everywhere. The streams are like invisible rays or beams. They are dangerous to living things and a human must be protected from the harm that the rays would do. Normally, the atmosphere filters the harmful rays, but in space a human must have protection. That is why an astronaut has to wear a space suit.

A space suit is actually a self-contained earth. Earth's atmosphere provides air to breathe and a space suit provides air to breathe. Again, the earth's atmosphere protects life from dangerous radiation. Likewise, a space suit is protection against radiation and other forms of energy, even little bits of "space sand," called *micrometeoroids*.

Eventually a person has to go to the bathroom and space suits are designed for that, too.

Very little gravity is found in space, away from the gravity of the earth or its moon, which means that a person floats around. This condition is known as *weightlessness*.

Humans are designed to live where there is air, gravity, water, food, light, and more. Regardless if trying to live in the ocean or out in space, a human must have some of these basics. So when you think of going out into space, think of "taking a little bit of planet earth along." It can be done, but take along special equipment.

THE FIRST STEP TO SPACE—THE ROCKET PLANE

Getting up and into space requires a craft that will travel very fast. Airplanes with propellers go fast, but not fast enough. A jet engine on an airplane makes it go faster, but the engine still needs oxygen to burn fuel. The jet must get oxygen from the air. Space does not have enough oxygen to do this. A craft that can take both fuel and oxygen is called a *rocket*.

Because rockets carry fuel and oxygen, they can go higher than a jet airplane. And because space is so much higher than the earth's atmosphere, rockets are used to get into space.

Back in the 1940s, a company known as Bell Aircraft developed an airplane powered by a rocket engine. The airplane was called the X-1. The X-1 was designed to go faster than the speed of sound (Fig. 6-1). The speed of sound is 1,100 feet per second, 760 miles per hour.

Fig. 6-1. The X-1 was designed to go faster than the speed of sound. Model by Revell.

Fig. 6-2. The X-15 was designed to conduct research on flight near the edge of space.

On October 14, 1947, Charles E. "Chuck" Yeager, flew the X-1 faster than the speed of sound. An airplane (or a rocket) that flies faster than the speed of sound is flying *supersonic*. Another term for the speed of sound is *Mach 1.0*. An airplane or rocket that is flying at Mach 3.5 is flying at three-and-a-half times the speed of sound.

TO THE EDGE OF SPACE IN THE X-15

The United States government organized the efforts of many groups in the 1950s into one space interest group that would become today's National Aeronautics and Space Administration, which most people call NASA. NASA's purpose is to conduct spaceflight research. One of the first programs to explore the edge of space relied on an aircraft known as the X-15. The X-15 was designed to conduct research on flight near the edge of space (Fig. 6-2).

One of the test pilots in the X-15 program was A. Scott Crossfield. He flew many test missions in the X-15. Scott Crossfield was also the first man to fly twice the speed of sound (Mach 2.0). The X-15 was the first aircraft to fly up into space and return, landing at Edwards Air Force Base, California. The remarkable research aircraft collected data on controllability, stability, heating caused by flying through the edge of the atmosphere, and high-speed aerodynamics. The X-15 eventually reached a speed of 4,534 miles per hour and achieved an altitude of 354,000 feet.

🛑 Figuring Mach number, and altitude in miles

(This task requires only pencil and paper, or a calculator.)

Perhaps you would like to determine the X-15's speed as a Mach number and the altitude in miles based on 4,534 miles per hour and 354,000 feet. Remember that the speed of sound is 760 miles per hour and a mile has 5,280 feet. Divide 4,534 by 760 for the Mach number. Divide 354,000 by 5,280 for the altitude in miles.

Those numbers help us understand space travel, but the same math can help us understand more about things closer to home.

Airline captains usually tell passengers the jetliner's altitude, which can be divided by 5,280 to determine the jetliner's altitude in miles: 33,000 feet divided by 5,280 feet equals 6.25 miles (which is above sea level, the figure is slightly less when the ground's elevation above sea level is subtracted).

Mountaintops are also measured in feet above sea level. Many mountains in Colorado, for example, are over 14,000 feet high. What is the result, in miles, after dividing 14,000 by 5,280? Find the highest point in your home state, usually on a road map prepared by the state government or in a state fact book, and do the division to determine the number of miles above sea level.

Finally, 60 miles per hour seems fast while riding in a car, but divide 60 by 760 (the speed of sound), to learn that the car is travelling only about Mach 0.08.

THE ROCKET

Rockets have been around for hundreds of years. The Chinese are given credit for the discovery of gunpowder. A primitive rocket was made by packing powder into a hollow tube and igniting the powder. Rockets were even used in early warfare, called *fire-arrows*, during the Chinese-Mongolian War of 1232.

By the 1700s, rockets were used in great numbers during major wars. Remember "rockets' red glare" in the United States' "National Anthem?" Francis Scott Key wrote this verse as a poem while watching a battle at Fort McHenry, Maryland, in September, 1814, during the War of 1812.

The early rockets were of a solid fuel type. This meant that the fuel and oxygen supply were mixed together. Once the rocket started to burn, there was not much chance to stop it.

A Russian scientist by the name of Konstantin Tsiolkovsky, developed ideas and theories about future rockets. He developed the mathematical formulas governing liquid fuel and multistage flights.

An American by the name of Robert H. Goddard, is given credit for being the father of modern rocketry. He was a professor at Clark University. He concentrated research on liquid fueled rockets using gasoline and liquid oxygen. He concluded that it was possible to achieve spaceflight by using multistaged rockets and the proper fuel and oxygen combination.

THE SPACE AGE

The Soviet Union launched the world's first satellite, called Sputnik I, into orbit on October 4, 1957. The United States launched its first satellite on January 31, 1958. There was great competition between the Soviet Union and the United States to see who could be first in space achievements.

Soviet cosmonaut Yuri Gagarin became the first human to fly up into space. His flight, on April 12, 1961, lasted 108 minutes and he orbited the earth one time. This flight proved that man could live and function in space.

America was not far behind, when, on May 5, 1961, the spacecraft with astronaut Alan Sheppard on board reached an altitude of 116 miles and traveled 302 miles forward. American astronaut John Glenn orbited the earth on February 20, 1962. NASA named America's first manned space program Project Mercury.

Several manned space programs followed. These included Project Gemini (two astronauts in one spacecraft) to conduct further research on space travel and Project Apollo (three astronauts in one spacecraft) to safely land on and return from the moon.

Finally, on July 20, 1969, astronaut Neil Armstrong stepped out of the Apollo 11 lunar landing spacecraft and set foot on the moon. His famous words were, "That's one small step for man, one giant leap for mankind."

America's first manned space station was called Skylab. It was a 100-ton cluster of units made up of a workshop and crew quarters. The crew helped gather data on earth resources and they conducted experiments to better understand living in space.

The United States and the Soviet Union cooperated on a joint space mission in 1975. America's Apollo spacecraft docked (with the help of a special docking collar) with the Soviet Union's Soyuz spacecraft as a gesture of goodwill and international cooperation regarding space research.

America launched the space shuttle Columbia on April 12, 1982. The mission lasted 54 hours. Columbia made history when it made a regular airplane-style landing on a runway at Edwards Air Force Base, California, where Chuck Yeager and Scott Crossfield and other pilots set so many records. Many shuttle flights have been launched and they continue today.

A tragedy occurred in 1986 when the Challenger shuttle exploded just after liftoff. All crewmembers were killed. The public was especially saddened because the first civilian to fly into space was a member of the crew. She was a teacher named Christa McAuliffe. Her mission on the shuttle was to conduct televised school lessons from space. The Challenger accident caused a temporary shutdown in America's manned space operations. When the cause of the explosion was discovered, other shuttles were changed and made safer.

The Civil Air Patrol's Cadet Program offers an excellent opportunity for young people to learn more about aerospace subjects. An excerpt from one of their publications takes a look at the space shuttle and its mission. Figure 6-3 shows the components of the shuttle orbiter. The fuel supply and solid rocket boosters are in Fig. 6-4.

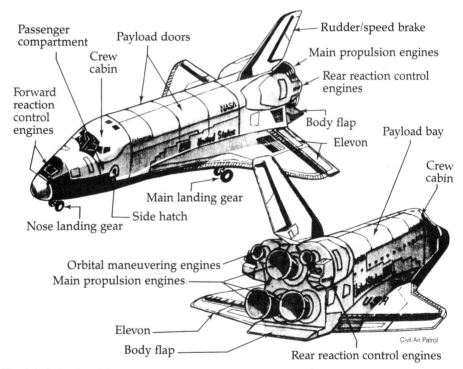

Fig. 6-3. A shuttle orbiter has many components.

The shuttle's mission is to transport payloads in a large bay area (Fig. 6-5) into space and help place the payloads into earth orbit and return for future missions. The orbiter must have crew and passenger compartments (Fig. 6-6). A typical shuttle mission (Fig. 6-7) might have single or multiple payloads (Fig. 6-8). One shuttle mission is to retrieve and service satellites that are already in orbit

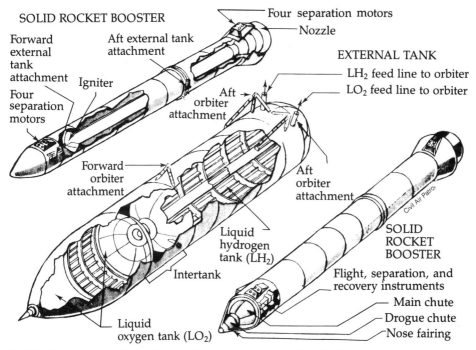

SOLID ROCKET BOOSTER

Four separation motors

Nozzle

Forward external tank attachment

Aft external tank attachment

EXTERNAL TANK

Igniter

LH₂ feed line to orbiter

LO₂ feed line to orbiter

Four separation motors

Aft orbiter attachment

Forward orbiter attachment

Aft orbiter attachment

SOLID ROCKET BOOSTER

Liquid hydrogen tank (LH₂)

Intertank

Flight, separation, and recovery instruments

Main chute

Drogue chute

Nose fairing

Liquid oxygen tank (LO₂)

Fig. 6-4. The space shuttle's solid rocket boosters and external fuel tank.

The payload bay can carry one or more satellites into space or can be used to bring satellites back to earth.

The payload bay is 15 feet in diameter and 60 feet long, and the orbiter can carry up to 65,000 pounds into orbit.

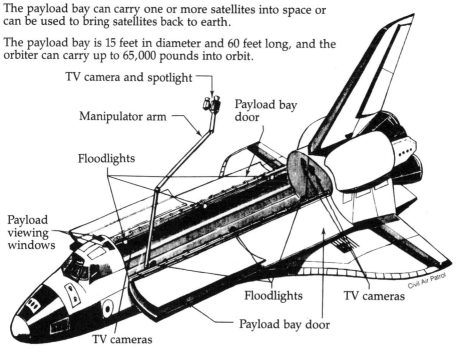

TV camera and spotlight

Manipulator arm

Payload bay door

Floodlights

Payload viewing windows

Floodlights

TV cameras

Payload bay door

TV cameras

Fig. 6-5. The payload bay is like the inside of a large moving van.

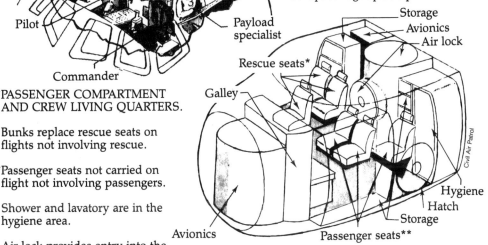

CREW

1. Shuttle commander: also operates the vehicle control station or the payload handling station in orbit.

2. Pilot: also operates the payload handling station in orbit.

3. Payload specialist

4. Mission specialist

5. Space flight participant

*PASSENGER COMPARTMENT AND CREW LIVING QUARTERS.

Bunks replace rescue seats on flights not involving rescue.

**Passenger seats not carried on flight not involving passengers.

Shower and lavatory are in the hygiene area.

Air lock provides entry into the payload bay.

Fig. 6-6. Crew and passenger compartments are found within the orbiter.

(Fig. 6-9). The orbiter also transports laboratories and crewmembers into earth orbit (Fig. 6-10).

Although a little advanced for the beginner, Estes makes a rocket-powered model of the space shuttle and it flies fantastic (Fig. 6-11). This model is especially realistic looking during liftoff.

The space program is active and plans are underway to build a permanent American space station (Fig. 6-12). There are also plans to travel to the moon again and eventually to Mars.

The space program is once again active and plans are being developed to build a permanent United States space station (Fig. 6-13). Also, plans are to go back to the moon and eventually go to Mars. Maybe you will be one of the first to set foot upon the mysterious red planet.

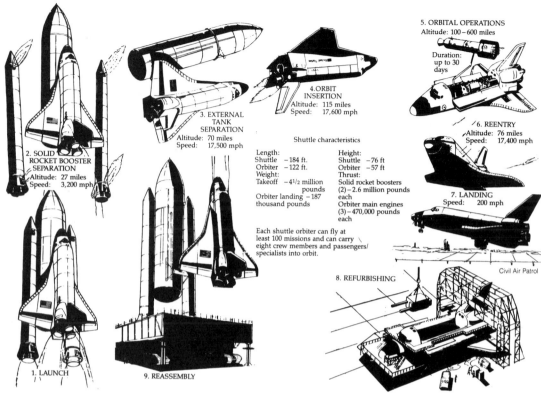

Fig. 6-7. A typical shuttle mission.

ROCKET PRINCIPLES

Mathematician Sir Isaac Newton developed three laws of science in the seventeenth century. He did not know it at the time, but these laws became the foundation for rocket flight:

- A body at rest, remains at rest unless acted upon by some outside force.
- A force acting upon a body causes (the body) to accelerate in the direction of the force.
- For every action, there is an equal and opposite reaction.

The third law is the basis of rocket power and can be demonstrated with a toy balloon.

🛑 Experimenting with Newton's third law

When you blow up a balloon, you are putting forces against the inside of the balloon, indicated by the black arrows in Fig. 6-14. If no air is allowed to escape, all of the forces—arrows—are equal. Now, if you let air escape at the opening of

This is the primary mission for the space shuttle. The orbiter can deliver up to 65,000 pounds into earth orbit. This may be one large satellite or up to five smaller ones.

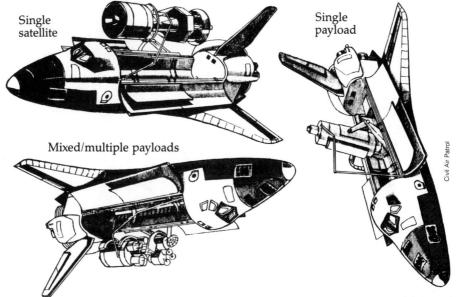

Single satellite

Single payload

Mixed/multiple payloads

Civil Air Patrol

The orbiter has a three-dimensional maneuvering capability. It can establish itself in any desired position in a specific orbit or it can change orbits.

Fig. 6-8. A shuttle can handle single and multiple payloads.

the balloon, the arrow at the opening becomes smaller because the pressure has been released (Fig. 6-15). The arrow at the opposite end is still the size it was when there was no air escaping. This means that the balloon will move in that direction, shown by the white arrow.

In terms of Newton's laws, the balloon is at rest and will stay at rest unless some force acts upon it. When the pressure is released at the open end of the balloon, the balloon moves in the opposite direction, or toward the arrow that is full sized. When the air rushes out the opening, this is called an action. The balloon shoots off in the other direction and this is a reaction.

A common misconception is that a rocket blast pushes against something to provide thrust. Wrong. Out in space where there is nothing to push against, a rocket actually works much better. Go back to the toy balloon and think about that arrow at the top of the balloon being full-size and the arrow at the opening being smaller—naturally, the balloon will move toward the larger arrow.

When the shuttle is sitting on the launch pad, it is loaded with fuel. The fuel contains *potential energy*. This means stored energy—it is rocket fuel and it is powerful. All of the force is stored in the fuel and is not used until the rocket is in flight.

When the fuel is ignited, it burns with oxygen. This causes a rapid expansion of the gases. This expansion is controlled through the rocket motor's nozzle and

The space shuttle is more than just a transport vehicle. The orbiter retrieves payloads from orbit and returns them to earth. Also, satellites are "plucked" out of space, repaired, and returned to orbit.

In-orbit servicing of satellites

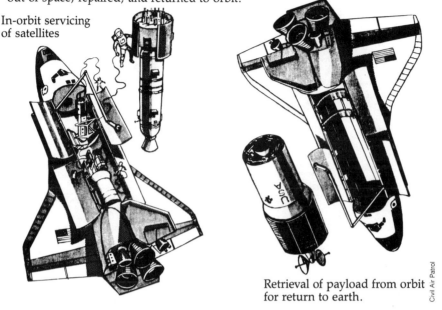

Retrieval of payload from orbit for return to earth.

Fig. 6-9. One shuttle mission is to retrieve and service satellites that are already in orbit.

spewed out the back. The potential energy of the rocket's fuel is now converted to *kinetic energy*. Kinetic energy is the energy of motion. When this kinetic energy moves in one direction, the rocket moves in the opposite direction.

Different rocket engines are available:

- If the fuel for the rocket is solid, like the Estes rocket model engines, it is a solid propellant rocket.
- If the fuel is separated into an oxidizer, such as liquid oxygen, and some other fuel, it is a liquid propellant rocket.
- Future rocket engines might include nuclear, electric, and photon.

Rocket performance is measured in several terms that you should understand:

- *Thrust* is the force that pushes the spacecraft, action in Newton's third law.
- *Reaction* is what the body of the rocket does when it moves.
- *Specific impulse* is the amount of thrust from each pound of fuel during one second of operation. (A measurement of the efficiency of a rocket fuel.)
- *Thrust-to-weight ratio* is the comparison between the thrust and weight of the rocket.

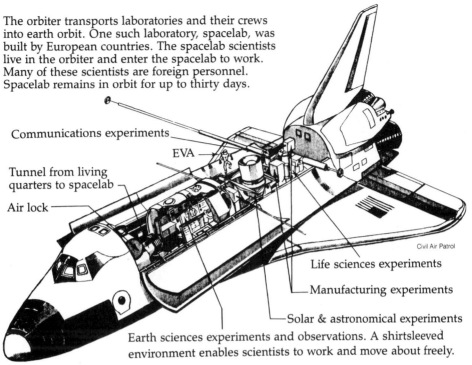

The orbiter transports laboratories and their crews into earth orbit. One such laboratory, spacelab, was built by European countries. The spacelab scientists live in the orbiter and enter the spacelab to work. Many of these scientists are foreign personnel. Spacelab remains in orbit for up to thirty days.

Communications experiments

EVA

Tunnel from living quarters to spacelab

Air lock

Civil Air Patrol

Life sciences experiments

Manufacturing experiments

Solar & astronomical experiments

Earth sciences experiments and observations. A shirtsleeved environment enables scientists to work and move about freely.

Fig. 6-10. The orbiter can transport laboratories and laboratory crews.

THE MODEL ROCKET

Thousands and thousands of model rockets are sold each year. Model rocketry is fun and educational. One company, Estes Industries, leads the way in producing safe and fun model rockets. Many aerospace enthusiasts have built model rockets, but many do not have clubs, schools, and other support to become active in the hobby. Here is one of the best models for the beginner or for the teacher who wants to have this as a class project. Instructions for the Alpha model rocket (Figs. 6-16A through 6-16D), reprinted courtesy Estes Industries, offer a basic understanding of everything to build the rocket.

THE NATIONAL AEROSPACE PLANE (NASP)

For years, scientists have imagined an airplane that could take off from a regular airport, then fly up into space, and finally return to a regular airport. The dream of such an air- and spacecraft is now becoming a fact. It is a radical new design that uses four engines to get it off the ground and up into space. The National Aerospace Plane (NASP) will be about 150 feet long and shaped similar to the paper airplane that you built and flew.

The space plane will have *turbojet* engines to get it off the ground and then speed up to Mach 2.0. Then *ramjet* engines will come on and push the speed up

Continued on page 101.

Fig. 6-11. Estes makes a rocket-powered model of the space shuttle for the experienced builder.

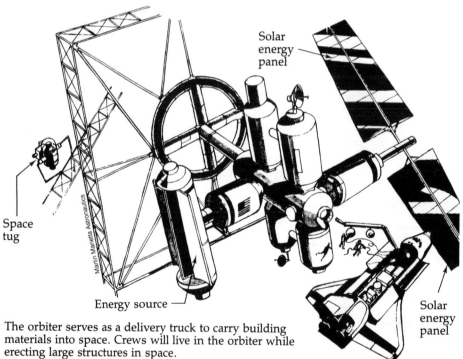

Martin Marietta Astronautics

Solar energy panel

Space tug

Energy source

Solar energy panel

The orbiter serves as a delivery truck to carry building materials into space. Crews will live in the orbiter while erecting large structures in space.

Fig. 6-12. The space program is active and a permanent United States space station is possible.

SPACE STATION

Legend
A. Vertical keel
B. Horizontal booms (upper and lower)
C. Transverse boom
D. Reaction control system
E. Photovoltaic (solar) cells
F. Solar dynamics generators
G. Habitation module
H. U.S. laboratory module
I. Japanese experiments module
J. European Space Agency module
K. Japanese logistics module
L. U.S. logistics module
M. Nodes
N. Service modules
O. Radiators
P. Canadian mobile sevicing center
Q. Free-flying platform

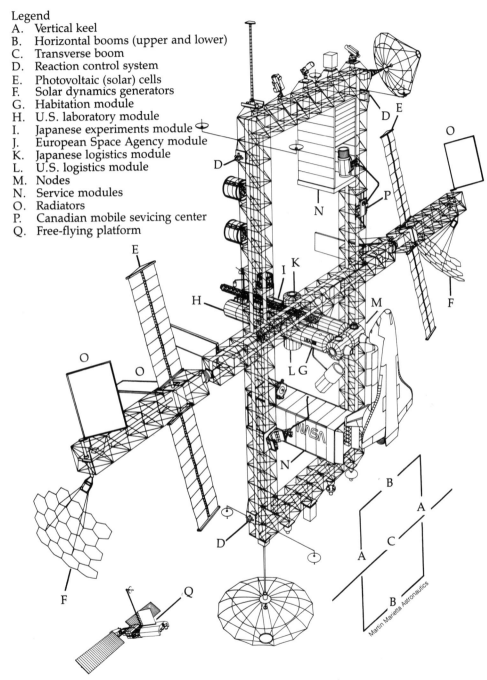

Fig. 6-13. A fully equipped space station would require many complex systems.

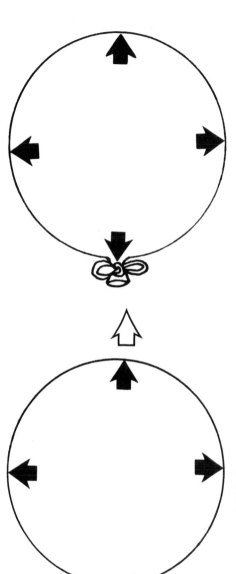

Fig. 6-14. An inflated balloon has compressed air pressing equally against all sides of the balloon from the inside.

Fig. 6-15. Air pressure inside a balloon decreases as shown by the small arrow when the compressed air rushes out of the open hole.

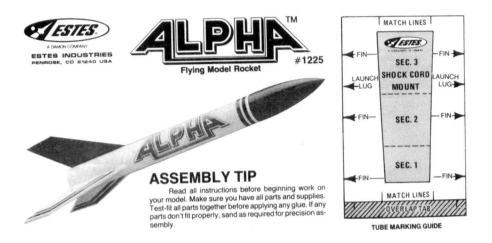

ASSEMBLY TIP

Read all instructions before beginning work on your model. Make sure you have all parts and supplies. Test-fit all parts together before applying any glue. If any parts don't fit properly, sand as required for precision assembly.

TUBE MARKING GUIDE

PARTS AND SUPPLIES

Locate the parts shown below and lay them out on the table in front of you. In addition to the parts included in the kit you will also need:

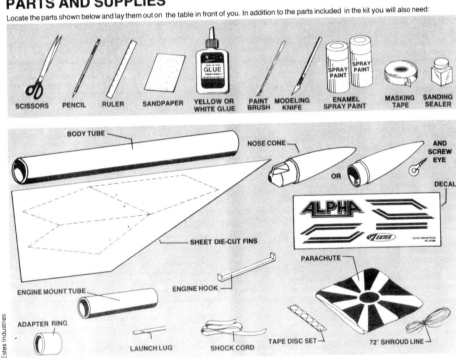

Estes Industries

Fig. 6-16A. Instructions for the Alpha flying model rocket provide a basic understanding of how to build and launch a rocket using the kit parts and supplies.

ROCKET ASSEMBLY

1

A. Mark engine mount tube 1 inch and 2½ inches from one end and then cut 1/8 inch long slit at 2½ inch mark.
B. Insert one end of engine hook into slit.
C. Slide adapter ring onto tube as shown to the 1 inch mark and then glue both ends of ring to tube.

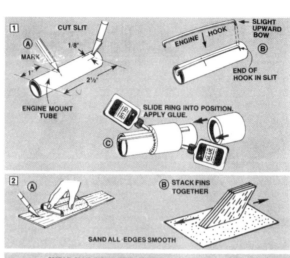

2

A. Fine sand balsa die-cut sheet. Carefully remove fins by freeing edges with sharp knife.
B. Stack fins together. Sand all edges smooth.

3

A. Using a piece of scrap balsa, smear glue inside body tube 1½ inches from one end.
B. Push engine mount in until tube ends are even.

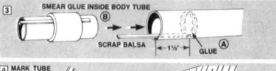

4

A. Cut out tube marking guide from front of instructions.
B. Wrap guide around the tube and mark tube at arrows. Remove guide and save.
C. Draw straight lines connecting each pair of marks.
D. Extend launch lug line 4" from rear of tube.

5

A. Lay fins on pattern to find front (leading) and gluing (root) edges.
B. Position and glue fins on alignment lines one at a time. Let each dry several minutes before applying the next one.
C. Adjust fins to project straight out from tube.
D. Do not set rocket on fins while glue is wet.

FINS MUST BE ATTACHED CORRECTLY FOR STABLE FLIGHT!

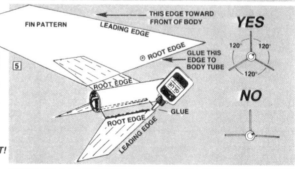

6

Glue launch lug straight on launch lug line 1¾" from rear of tube.

Fig. 6-16B.

7

A. Cut shock cord mount from tube marking guide.
B. Crease on dotted lines by folding. Spread glue on section 1 and lay end of shock cord into glue. Fold over and apply glue to back of first section and exposed part of section 2 . Lay shock cord as shown with fingers and fold mount over again.
C. Clamp unit together with fingers until glue sets.

8

A. Apply glue to inside front of body tube to cover an area no less than 1" to 2" from end. The glued area should be same size as shock cord mount.
B. Press mount firmly onto inside of tube.
C. Hold until glue sets.

9

A. Apply a glue reinforcement to each fin/ body tube joint and each side of launch lug.
B. Support rocket as shown until glue dries.

10

Trim excess plastic from around sides of nose cone with a sharp knife. Also remove any excess plastic from inside molded eyelet. Wipe nose cone with damp cloth to remove oil and dirt.
OR
Install screw eye by twisting into molded nose cone boss. Turn screw eye parallel to side of nose cone.

11

A. Cut out parachute on edge lines.
B. Cut three 23" lengths of shroud line.
C. Form small loops with shroud line ends and press onto sticky side of tape discs.
D. Attach tape discs with line ends to top of parachute as shown.
E. Firmly press tape discs into place until both tape discs and parachute material are molded around shroud line loops.
F. Pass shroud line loops through eyelet on nose cone. Pass parachute through loop ends and pull lines against the nose cone.
G. Tie free end of shock cord to nose cone loop.

Estes Industries

Fig. 6-16C.

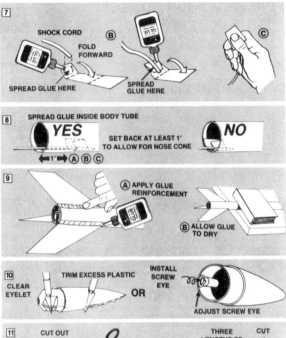

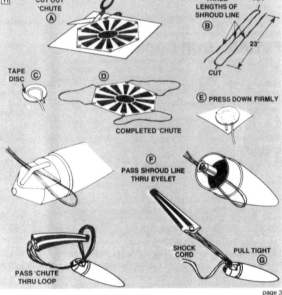

page 3

FINISHING YOUR ROCKET

Apply sanding sealer to wood parts with small brush. When sealer is dry, lightly sand all sealed surfaces. Repeat sealing and sanding until balsa grain is filled and smooth. When sanding sealer and glue are completely dry, paint model with spray enamel. Follow instructions on spray can for best results. Let paint dry overnight before masking to paint second color. To

apply decals, cut each out, dip in lukewarm water for 20 seconds, and hold until it uncurls. Refer to photograph on front page and/or on front of panel for decal placement. Slip decal off backing sheet and onto model. Blot away excess water. For best results, let decals dry overnight, and apply a coat of clear spray paint to protect decals.

ROCKET PREFLIGHT

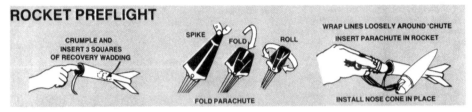

CRUMPLE AND INSERT 3 SQUARES OF RECOVERY WADDING

SPIKE
FOLD
ROLL

FOLD PARACHUTE

WRAP LINES LOOSELY AROUND 'CHUTE
INSERT PARACHUTE IN ROCKET

INSTALL NOSE CONE IN PLACE

PREPARE ENGINE

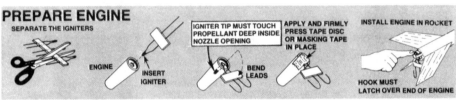

SEPARATE THE IGNITERS

ENGINE

INSERT IGNITER

IGNITER TIP MUST TOUCH PROPELLANT DEEP INSIDE NOZZLE OPENING

APPLY AND FIRMLY PRESS TAPE DISC OR MASKING TAPE IN PLACE

BEND LEADS

INSTALL ENGINE IN ROCKET

HOOK MUST LATCH OVER END OF ENGINE

LAUNCH SUPPLIES

To launch your rocket you will need the following items:
—Estes Electrical Launch System and Launch Pad
—Estes Recovery Wadding (No. 2274)
—Recommended Estes Engines: 1/2A6-2, A8-3, A8-5, B4-4, B4-6, B6-4, B6-6, B8-5, C6-5, or C6-7
To become familiar with your rocket's flight pattern, use an A8-3 engine for your first flight.
Use only Estes products to launch this rocket.

FLYING YOUR ROCKET

Choose a large field away from power lines, tall trees, and low flying aircraft. Try to find a field at least 250 feet square. The larger the launch area, the better your chance of recovering your rocket. Football fields and playgrounds are great.
Launch area must be free of dry weeds and brown grass.
Launch only during calm weather with little or no wind and good visibility.
Don't leave parachute packed more than a minute or so before launch during cold weather [colder than 40° Fahrenheit (4° Celsius)].
Parachute may be dusted with talcum powder to avoid sticking

MISFIRES

Failure of the model rocket engine to ignite is nearly always caused by incorrect igniter installation. An Estes igniter will function properly even if the coated tip is chipped. However, if the coated tip is not in direct contact with the engine propellant, it will only heat and not ignite the engine.
When an ignition failure occurs, remove the safety key from the launch control system, and wait one minute before approaching the rocket. Remove the expended igniter from the engine, and install a new one. Be certain the coated tip is in direct contact with the engine propellant, then tape the igniter leads firmly to base of engine as illustrated above. Repeat the countdown and launch procedure.

FOR YOUR SAFETY AND ENJOYMENT

Always follow the NAR-HIA* MODEL ROCKETRY SAFETY CODE while participating in any model rocketry activities.

*National Association of Rocketry-The Hobby Industry of America

COUNTDOWN AND LAUNCH

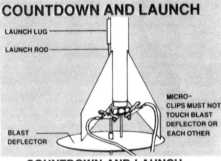

LAUNCH LUG

LAUNCH ROD

MICRO-CLIPS MUST NOT TOUCH BLAST DEFLECTOR OR EACH OTHER

BLAST DEFLECTOR

COUNTDOWN AND LAUNCH

(10) REMOVE SAFETY KEY to disarm the launch controller.

(9) Remove safety cap and slide launch lugs over launch rod to place rocket on launch pad. Make sure the rocket slides freely on the launch rod.

(8) Attach micro-clips to the igniter wires. Arrange the clips so they do not touch each other or the metal blast deflector. Attach clips as close to protective tape on igniter as possible.

(7) Move back from your rocket as far as launch wire will permit (at least 15 feet).

(6) INSERT SAFETY KEY to arm the launch controller.

Give audible countdown 5...4...3...2...1

LAUNCH!!! PUSH AND HOLD LAUNCH BUTTON UNTIL ENGINE IGNITES

Remove safety key---Replace cap on launch rod.

82925G

Estes Industries

Fig. 6-16D.

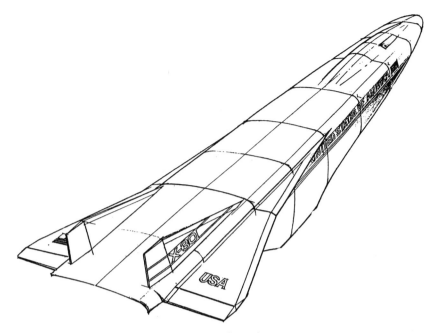

Fig. 6-17. The X-30 National Aerospace Plane configuration.

to about Mach 8.0 (760 × 8). Once Mach 8.0 is attained *scramjet* engines will take over and propel the NASP up to Mach 20.0 (760 × 20). Finally, pure rocket engines will put the aircraft into orbit at Mach 25.0, approximately 18,000 miles per hour (Fig. 6-17).

One of the biggest problems facing the NASP is heat. Heat is generated not only during climb, but during descent back into the atmosphere. The scientists are planning to make the skin of the NASP out of an alloy (mixture) of titanium and aluminum. Other components will be made of heat-resistant carbon compounds. Because cold liquid hydrogen is going to be used for fuel, scientists are also thinking about using it to help cool the skin. This will be done by building a collection of pipes near the surface to help carry away the heat. Hydrogen is extremely cold in the liquid form and would be an excellent coolant for the excess heat. Liquid hydrogen has a temperature of −423°F. Temperatures on the skin of the aerospace plane might exceed 4,000°F.

The NASP will be a completely reusable aerospace craft. At first, it will be used for research. When scientists get all of the bugs worked out, it might eventually be used to carry passengers to all parts of the world. Someday you might fly into space and back again in an aerospace craft much like the National Aerospace Plane.

🛑 Building the National Aerospace Plane

Although we can't build a model that has turbojets, ramjets, scramjets, and rocket engines like the NASP, we can build a neat static model that looks like it. These are the supplies that you will need for the model:

- A cardboard tube.
- 3 sheets of balsa wood. We used 2 sheets of $1/2 \times 3 \times 12$ inches and 1 sheet of $3/32 \times 4 \times 36$ inches.
- You will need sandpaper. We used one sheet of #80 grit and one sheet of #100 grit. The sandpaper can be found at hardware stores.
- A tube of wood glue is needed. We used a brand-name cement for wood models. We also used some rubber cement to glue the paper side-view of the NASP to the balsa plank.
- A pair of scissors, a coping saw, and an hobby knife or a single-edge razor blade is needed for trimming and cutting the paper and balsa wood.

An advanced builder can make this NASP model rocket powered. If you are interested, ask for help from your local hobby shop or club that specializes in model rockets. Let's get started.

1. An adult with access to a photocopy machine should help you with this step. Lay Fig. 6-18 down on the machine and enlarge the illustration until the side-view is about one foot long. This will bring the rest of the plans up to the proper size for the project.
2. Figure 6-19 shows the basic way the NASP model is going to go together.
3. Figure 6-20 shows how an advanced modeler might put a rocket motor in a model of the X-30. Remember that only an experienced rocket modeler should attempt to build a rocket-powered model. This requires extensive testing and skills.
4. Lay out the enlarged three-view of the NASP and cut out the side-view of the fuselage. The side-view is glued to the $1/2$-inch balsa plank shown. This will be the side of the aircraft and you will have to cut it out using a hobby saw.
5. Next, make a sanding block using a piece of hard, flat wood, and (preferred) sticky-back sandpaper.
6. The sides of the fuselage are now shaped using the sanding block.
7. Once the general shape is correct to the side view, the two halves are glued to a paper tube (Fig. 6-21).
8. A thin piece of balsa is glued to the upper fuselage.
9. A similar piece is glued to the lower portion of the fuselage.
10. The vertical stabilizers and wings are now made using the plans showing the top and sideview. These are cut and glued into position (Fig. 6-22).
11. The next step to is to round off the edges and make the NASP look like the real one. Using #60–80 grit sandpaper, round off the edges and

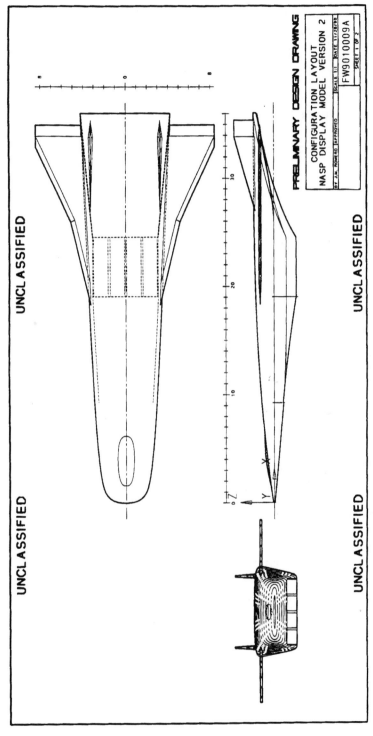

Fig. 6-18. An adult with access to a photocopy machine that can enlarge can help you enlarge this drawing to make parts for a space plane model.

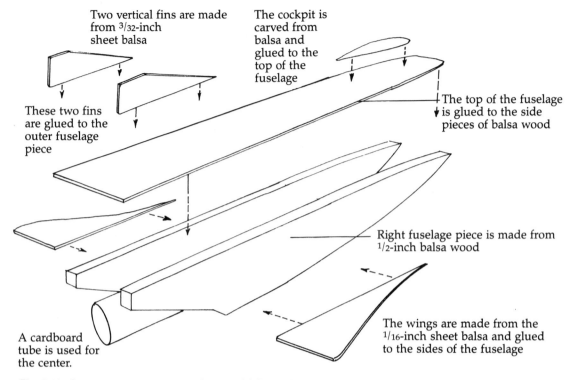

Two vertical fins are made from 3/32-inch sheet balsa

The cockpit is carved from balsa and glued to the top of the fuselage

These two fins are glued to the outer fuselage piece

The top of the fuselage is glued to the side pieces of balsa wood

Right fuselage piece is made from 1/2-inch balsa wood

A cardboard tube is used for the center.

The wings are made from the 1/16-inch sheet balsa and glued to the sides of the fuselage

Fig. 6-19. Components of the space plane model fit together over a model rocket body.

shape the body to look like the three-view drawings and actual photographs (Fig. 6-23).

12. The fuselage is now shaped from the top view using a sanding block.

13. The X-30 model is now coated with a balsa wood filler that may be purchased at local hobby shops.

14. Check the model to make sure everything is in place and construction is complete.

15. Paint the aircraft in white and blue, with red trim (Fig. 6-24), or design a personalized color scheme. If this is a project in science class, perhaps the school colors would be appropriate (Figures 6-25 and 6-26).

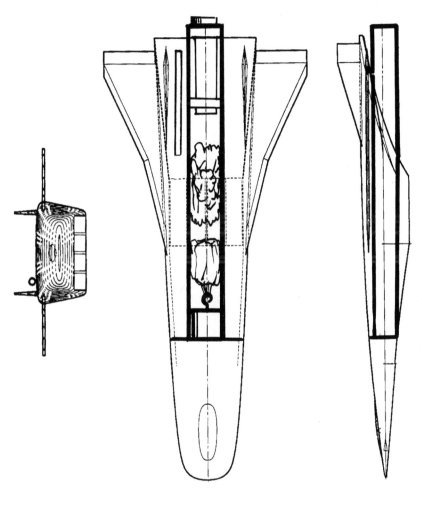

Fig. 6-20. An advanced modeler could build the X-30 with rocket power complete with parachute recovery.

Fig. 6-21. Two halves are glued to the rocket tube.

Fig. 6-22. The wings are glued into position.

Fig. 6-23. The fuselage is shaped with a sanding block.

Fig. 6-24. The model may be painted with a patriotic red, white, and blue.

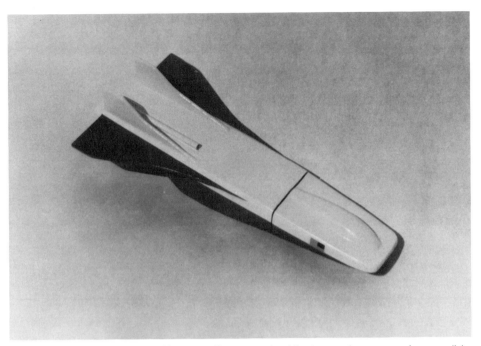

Fig. 6-25. The NASP X-30 model is an excellent example of the tremendous sense of accomplishment when learning about aerospace science.

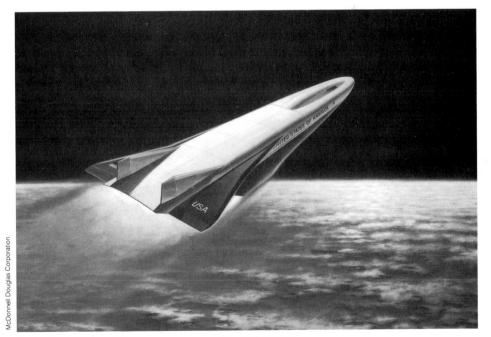

McDonnell Douglas Corporation.

Fig. 6-26. America's future in aerospace is the NASP X-30.

FLYING SAUCERS

One of the most popular forms of flying toys is the Frisbee. This became popular nearly 40 years ago when there was great interest in flying saucers. A Frisbee is a rotating flying disk that achieves a small amount of lift from thrust (thrown by a person) and rotation (flipped by the thrower's hand, wrist, and elbow when released). When the edge of a Frisbee rotates and moves forward, the relative wind moves up and over the edge, and the pressure drops (Fig. 6-27), creating lift, and it flies. The direction of the spinning disk is determined by tilt, commonly applied by the thrower's hand; the disc is tilted downward when released and it curves in that direction. No tilt means a straight flight. Any one of several models (Fig. 6-28) may be thrown in games of catch, Frisbee football, or Frisbee golf at specially laid out courses in parks.

Flying saucers are fun to fly. Who knows, someday the attention of the world will be turned to the first flying saucer that lands on earth. Won't that be something!

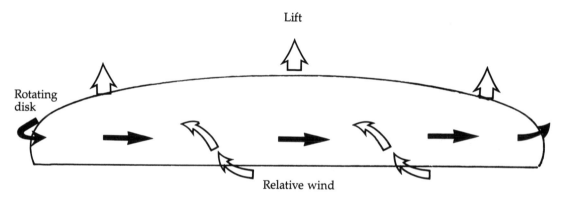

Fig. 6-27. A flying disc creates lift when spun and thrown by a person. Recall that lift occurs where the air pressure is reduced.

Fig. 6-28. Most toy and hobby stores have many varieties of flying discs and similar flying toys.

Resources

WHERE DO YOU WRITE when you want to find out more about aviation and space? This has been a chronic problem for students, parents, and teachers, until now because this appendix tells you where to get all kinds of materials, and most of the materials are free.

A LETTER BY YOU, TO THEM

First, here is a form letter to write for materials. All you have to do is copy the letter with your information inserted as noted, and mail it directly to the company. I have tried to make the letter short and to the point.

Big companies often have a special office to help people with information. The office is called *public relations* or *public affairs*. A letter addressed directly to the proper office will get to the correct person faster.

It is easy because all you have to do is use the form letter, the company address, and your information. Hand printing or typing the letter on a typewriter or computer will help appearance.

Continued on page 112.

Letter Contents

Your name
Your address
Your city, state, and zip code

Date of the letter

Office of Public Affairs
Company name
Company address
Company city, state, and zip code

Dear Sir:

My name is _____ and I am a student at _____ (the name of your school). I am doing a class project and would like to have your help. I found your address in the book *Aviation and Space Science Projects,* by Dr. Ben Millspaugh.

The subject of my project is _____ (the name of your subject and project). I have to have my project finished and handed in by _____ (the date that your assignment is due).

I was wondering if you would please send me _____ (talk to your teacher and parents to determine what you really need from the company and make a precise request: photos, information brochures, catalog, prices, and the like).

If you have any other materials that you think might help me with this project, I would appreciate receiving them.

Thank you for helping.

Sincerely,

(Your signature)

HELPFUL HINTS

If you have the name of a person who works in the public affairs office, address the letter directly to him or her; it will usually get quicker results.

Again, if you can write the letter on a typewriter or computer, do it.

If you do not know how to type, or cannot find someone to do it for you, print the letter. Everyone has different cursive handwriting and some handwriting is difficult to read.

Sometimes it is a good idea for a parent or a teacher to also sign the letter. This tells the company that you really are doing a school project and not just looking for free stuff.

MODELS

Midwest Products Co., Inc.
400 S. Indiana St., P.O. Box 564, Hobart, IN 46342
(Delta Dart, Flash X-18, Flip Glider, Rogue, Star Glider, and Tech Twin. Catalog is free.)

Chuck Larsen
Educational Director
E.A.A. Educational Division
Wittman Field, Oshkosh, WI 54903-3065
(Materials on Flip glider, building airplane wing ribs, airplane instrument bracket, paper airplanes, hot-air balloon models, flight simulators, flight trainer, control surface demonstration models.)

Space Age Distributing Co.
4888 Cedar Ridge N.E., Grand Rapids, MI 49505
(Hot-air balloon kit.)

Academy of Model Aeronautics
1810 Samuel Morse Drive, Reston, VA 22090
(Information about model planes in general. This is a national organization of model builders and flyers.)

Estes Industries
P.O. Box 227, Penrose, CO 81240
(Model rockets and related educational materials.)

Revell, Inc.
4288 Glencoe Ave., Venice, CA 90291
(Model aircraft and spacecraft.)

Flight Systems, Inc.
9300 E. 68th St., Raytown, MO 64133
(Model rockets.)

Pacific Miniatures, Inc.
817 S. Palm Ave., Alhambra, CA 91803
(Model rockets.)

Monogram Models, Inc.
Morton Grove, IL 90053
(Plastic model spacecraft.)

Custom Graphics
P.O. Box 2176, Altamonte Springs, FL 32715

Toys & Models Corp.
222 River St., Hackensack, NJ 07601

Wesco Models, Inc.
1453 J. Virginia Ave., Baldwin Park, CA 91706

Scale Models, Inc.
111 Independence Dr., Menlo Park, CA 94025

Movie Miniatures
5115 Douglas Fir Drive, Suite F, Calabasas, CA 91302

Windseeker, Inc.
Sugar Hill Road, Falls Village, CT 06031
(Windseeker hang glider model.)

Schylling Associates, Inc.
P.O. Box 233, Peabody, MA 01960
(Flying Bird ornithopter.)

Paper Airplanes
433 Nihoa St., Kahului, Hawaii 96732
(Flying paper airplanes: A-10, F-4, F-16, F/A 18, and F-15.)

Silver Star Systems
6228 S. Forest Court, Littleton, CO 80121
(Silver Star Sleeper flying model airplane.)

Into The Wind
1408 Pearl, Boulder, CO 80302
(Store with everything that flies.)

Sky Flyer, Inc.
P.O. Box 19-7815, St. Paul, Minnesota 55119
(Hi-Flight helicopter.)

SOUVENIRS AND MEMORABILIA

American's interest in aviation and space has spawned many books, photo albums, emblems, patches, decals, flight jackets, T-shirts, caps, buttons, and the like:

AW/JSC Exchange Store
Johnson Space Center
Houston, TX 77058

Alabama Space & Rocket Center
Tranquility Base
Huntsville, AL 35807

Space Age Enterprises
P.O. Box 58127, Houston, TX 77058

National Medallion Co., Inc.
P.O. Box 58127, Houston, TX 77058

KSC Tours
TWA Services
TWA-810
Kennedy Space Center, FL 32889

Communications Association Corp.
250 Babcock St., Melbourne, FL 32935

Smithsonian Institution Museum Shops
900 Jefferson Drive SW, Washington, DC 20560

NASA Headquarters Exchange Store
600 Maryland Ave. SW, Washington, DC 20546

Action Packets
344 Cypress Road, Ocala, FL 32672

International Space Hall of Fame Gift Shop
P.O. Box 25, Alamogordo, NM 88310

GEWA Gift Shop
Goddard Space Flight Center
Greenbelt, MD 20771

Space Art Original Paintings & Prints
Blatch Museum
P.O. Box 584, Rockledge, FL 32955-0584

Wag-Aero
P.O. Box 181, 1216 N. Road, Lyons, WI 53148
(This mail-order company has tons of neat aviation and airplane stuff. Every aviation enthusiast enjoys looking through their catalog.)

Aero-Gem Shirts
P.O. Box 521238, Miami, FL 33152-1238
(Airline logos.)

Johnson and Associates
Pentagon
P.O. Box 46251, Washington, DC 20050

SPACE SUITS

ILC-Dover
P.O. Box 266, Frederica, DE 19946
(Information about space suits and artificial environments.)

Hamilton Standard
Windsor Locks, CT 06096
(Information about space suits.)

STAMPS

Johnson Space Center Stamp Club
P.O. Box 58328, Houston, TX 77058

Houston Hobby Center
P.O. Box 10791, Houston, TX 77018

GEWA Visitor Center Gift Shop
Goddard Space Flight Center
Greenbelt, MD 20771

CAMPS AND SPECIAL PROGRAMS

Chuck Larsen
Aviation Education
Experimental Aircraft Association
Wittman Field, Oshkosh, WI 54903-3065
(Aviation-oriented summer programs. Brochures are free.)

Space Camp
Alabama Space & Rocket Center
Tranquility Base
Huntsville, AL 35807
(Camps and academy training for 10-year-old through adult students.)

Earth Shuttle
The Carter Company of Boston, Inc.
11 Beacon St., Boston, MA 02108
(Aerospace weekends for all students in grades 3–12. Includes classes, private
briefings, activities, and in-depth tours. Brochures are free.)

Robin Stoddard
Wright Flight, Inc.
1300 East Valencia Road #300, Tucson, AZ 85706
(A program aimed at helping students improve in school by becoming involved
in flight training.)

Explorer Programs
Boy Scouts of America
1325 Walnut Hill Lane, Irving, TX 75038-3096
(Explorers offers career investigation programs in cooperation with aviation and

aerospace companies. Students in the greater Denver area meet at United Airlines and Martin Marietta Astronautics once a month. Meeting programs commonly include a guest speaker or a tour.)

Civil Air Patrol
Cadet Program
Maxwell AFB, AL 33112-5872
(Camps are part of the summer activities for cadets.)

Pacific Rim Spaceflight Academy
Oregon Museum of Science and Industry
4015 SW Canyon Road, Portland, OR 97221
(Ages 8 – 10; 11 – 13; and 14 – 16.)

Future Astronaut Training Program
Kansas Cosmosphere and Space Center
1100 North Plum, Hutchinson, KS 67501
(Grades 7 – 9.)

Shuttle Camp
Space Center
P.O. Box 533, Alamogordo, NM 88311-0533
(Grades 3 – 9.)

Flight Camp
Pacific Science Center
200 Second Ave. North, Seattle, WA 98109
(Ages 9 – 12.)

Southern New Jersey Space Education Camp
South New Jersey Chamber Foundation
North Park Drive, Pennsanken, NJ 08109
(Local students, ages 12 and 13.)

Mississippi Student Space Station
Russell C. Davis Planetarium
P.O. Box 22826, Jackson, MS 39225-2826
(Middle and senior high school students, also teachers.)

Sky-Life Foundation, Inc.
P.O. Box 839, Northville, NY 12134
(Middle and high school students.)

University of North Dakota
Department of Aviation
University Station, P.O. Box 8216, Grand Forks, ND 58202
(Middle and high school students.)

ASSOCIATIONS

Aerospace Industries Association of America, Inc.
1250 Eye St. NW, Washington, DC 20005
(Information on aerospace manufacturing, including aircraft, missiles, space-craft, helicopters, and equipment.)

Air Line Pilots Association
1625 Massachusetts Ave. NW, Washington, DC 20036
(Education, safety, and pilot career information.)

Air Traffic Control Association
220 N. 14th St., Suite 410, Arlington, VA 22201
(Information on national air traffic control.)

Air Transport Association of America
1709 New York Ave. NW, Washington, DC 20006
(Information on the scheduled airline industry.)

Aircraft Electronics Association
P.O. Box 1961, Independence, MO 64055
(Information on the installation of airplane radios.)

Aircraft Owners and Pilots Association
421 Aviation Way, Frederick, MD 21701
(Information on general aviation regulations, safety, and community airports.)

American Institute of Aeronautics & Astronautics
370 L'Enfant Promenade SW, Washington, DC 20024
(Educational material on aeronautics and astronautics.)

Animal Air Transportation Association
P.O. Box 441110, Fort Washington, MD 20744
(Information on the methods and services for national and international air transportation of animals.)

Aviation Distributors and Manufacturers Association
1900 Arch St., Philadelphia, PA 19103
(Information on aviation products, distributors, and educational materials related to aviation.)

Aviation Maintenance Foundation, Inc.
P.O. Box 2826, Redmond, WA 98073
(Vocational guidance, books, and technical materials.)

Civil Air Patrol
Building 714, Maxwell AFB, AL 33112-5872
(Aerospace education programs and materials. CAP is an auxiliary of the United States Air Force.)

Experimental Aircraft Association
Educational Division
Wittman Field, Oshkosh, WI 54903-3086
(Information on building airplanes, kitplanes, sport aviation, antique and warplane restoration, aviation camps, and summer academy programs.)

Federal Aviation Administration
Aviation Education APA-100
800 Independence Ave. SW, Washington, DC 20591
(Information on all facets of aviation. The FAA offers a tremendous amount of aviation educational material, as well as films and audiovisual aids for teachers.)

General Aviation Manufacturers Association
1400 K St. NW, Suite 801, Washington, DC 20005
(Information on general aviation statistics, learning to fly, teaching, and the manufacture of airplanes.)

Jeppesen-Sanderson
55 Inverness Drive East, Englewood, CO 80112
(Textbooks, overhead projection materials, video cassettes, and more about learning to fly.)

National Aeronautics and Space Administration
Educational Programs Office
600 Independence Ave., Washington, DC 20548
(Information on career opportunities and educational materials relating to space.)

National Agricultural Aviation Association
115 D St. SE, Suite 103, Washington, DC 20003
(Materials and information on agricultural aviation.)

National Air Transportation Association
4226 King St., Alexandria, VA 22302
(Information on airport service organizations, air charter, and flight training.)

National Association of Air Traffic Specialists
4780 Corridor Place, Beltsville, MD 20705
(Information on careers in air traffic control.)

National Transportation Safety Board
Office of Public Affairs
800 Independence Ave. SW, Washington, DC 20591
(Information on air traffic safety and accident investigation.)

The Ninety-Nines, Inc.
Will Rogers World Airport, P.O. Box 59965, Oklahoma City, OK 73159
(An organization of women pilots that helps promote aviation through national activities.)

Soaring Society of America, Inc.
P.O. Box E, Hobbs, NM 88241
(Information about gliders and soaring.)

United States Hang Glider Association
P.O. Box 8300, Colorado Springs, CO 80933

4-H Aerospace Education
National 4-H Program
U.S. Dept of Agriculture
Room 38605, Washington, DC 20250
(An outreach program for projects in aviation and space.)

Air Force Office of Youth Relations
Kelly AFB, TX 78241-5000
(Information about the Air Force.)

Air Transport Association of America
Public Relations Committee
1709 New York Ave. NW, Washington, DC 20006
(Information about airlines and airline-related industries.)

American Helicopter Society, Inc.
217 North Washington St., Alexandria, VA 22314
(Information about helicopters and related subjects.)

Aircraft Electronics Association
P.O. Box 1981, Independence, MO 64055
(Information about aircraft radios and navigation electronics.)

Cessna Aircraft Company
Air Age Education
P.O. Box 1521, Wichita, KS 67201
(Information about aviation, the company, and company products.)

Challenger Center for Space Science Education
Education Department
1101 King St., Suite 190, Alexandria, VA 22314
(Information about space and space-related subjects.)

National Air and Space Museum
Public Relations Department
7th St. and Independence Ave. SW, Washington, DC 20560
(Information about aviation and space history.)

Unique Patchwork Kites
Attn: Scott R. Skinner
Suite 406, Alamo Building, 128 S. Tejon St.
Colorado Springs, CO 80903

United States Space Foundation
P.O. Box 1838, Colorado Springs, CO 80901
(Information about space-related subjects.)

National Space Society
922 Pennsylvania Ave. SE, Washington, DC 20003
(Information about space-related subjects.)

NASA
Educational Affairs Division
Code XEO, NASA Headquarters
Washington, DC 20546
(Information about space-related subjects.)

National Association of State Aviation Officials
Metro Plaza One, Suite 505, 8401 Colesville Road, Silver Spring, MD 20910
(Information about state aviation departments and materials that might be available.)

The Young Astronaut Council
Suite 800, 1211 Connecticut Ave. NW, Washington, DC 20036
(Information about the council's youth astronaut program.)

TELL YOUR TEACHER AND PARENTS

The NASA Mobile Teacher Resource Center is a 22-ton tractor/trailer that contains lesson plans, slides, and videotapes on aeronautics, astronomy, and space exploration. Teachers may copy this material for classroom use. This project is aimed at reaching teachers who might not have access to similar resource centers at NASA field offices. The object of the mobile resource center is to get materials into the hands of teachers and help them teach mathematics and science:
Public Affairs Office
George C. Marshall Space Flight Center
Huntsville, AL 35812.

The National Congress On Aviation and Space Education is an annual convention for teachers, administrators, counselors, and others involved in aerospace education. It is sponsored by the Civil Air Patrol, NASA, and the FAA. If you have a teacher who is interested in aviation or space, this is a convention for learning new ideas about using the fascination of flight in the classroom. The average attendance exceeds 1,000 educators:
CAP National Headquarters
Building 714, Maxwell AFB, AL 36112-5572.

Space Calendar is a weekly newsletter by subscription devoted to listing space education resources available to teachers:
Space Age Publishing Company
3210 Scott Boulevard, Santa Clara, CA 95054-0975

Final Frontier is a space exploration bimonthly magazine by subscription:
P.O. Box 20089, Minneapolis, MN 55420-2089

Aviation Education Newsletter is a monthly newsletter devoted to teachers of aviation- and space-related subjects from kindergarten through college:
1000 Connecticut Ave. NW Suite 9, Washington, DC 20036

Educator News is a newsletter about using model rocketry as a teaching aid in the classroom:
Estes Industries, P.O. Box 227, Penrose, CO 81240

Jeppesen-Sanderson is one of the leaders in the field of aviation education with a wide assortment of books and audiovisual materials available for teaching aviation in schools:
Jeppesen-Sanderson
55 Inverness Drive East, Englewood, CO 80112-5498

Challenger Center has materials available to teachers for aerospace education in grades K-12:
Challenger Center for Space Science Education
Education Department
1101 King St., Suite 190, Alexandria, VA 22314

A teacher activity book is available that gives teachers aviation related projects to use in the elementary and middle school classroom:
Academy of Model Aeronautics

Beechcraft offers a complete package of aviation education modules for teachers. Each module contains background information, objectives, and activities printed in a folder. Information and activity sheets are included for teachers and students:
Beech Aircraft Corporation
Aviation Education Division
9709 East Central, Wichita, KS 67201

An FAA booklet explains many education programs and associated information (Air Bear Program; Airway Science Instruction Program; Young Artist Contest; International Science and Engineering Fair; Youth Career Education Academy; Aviation Education Resource Centers; National Congress; Administrator's Awards for Excellence; Cooperative Education Program; Stay-in-School Program; Historically Black Colleges and Universities; Federal Junior Fellowship Program; Airway Science Curriculum Program; Airway Science Grant Program; Aviation Education Materials Listing; and Aviation Education Materials Order Forms):
Aviation Education Programs and Materials Booklet
APA-156
Federal Aviation Administration
800 Independence Ave. SW, Washington, DC 20591

Teachers may attend a nationally recognized workshop and earn graduate credit from Colorado State University. Workshop instructors have won two or more national awards in aerospace education. Workshops are usually five days long and are conducted during the summer in Denver or at the Air Force Academy in Colorado Springs:

Wings of Fame
Aerospace Education Workshops for Teachers
P.O. Box 8001, Englewood, CO 80110

Goodyear may be contacted for information about the blimps:

Richard F. Sailer, Manager
Airship Public Relations
Dept. 798-R-3
Goodyear Tire & Rubber Company
Akron, OH 44316-0001

Glossary

ENGLISH-SPANISH

aileron Control surfaces hinged at the back of the wings which by deflecting up or down helps to bank the airplane.

alerón Plano de control abisagrado, en la parte posterior del ala, el que al moverse hacia arriba o hacia abajo, ayuda a inclinar al avión en forma lateral.

airplane A mechanically-driven, fixed-wing, heavier-than-air craft.

avión, aeronave Máquina voladora, impulsada por medios mecánicos, de alas fijas y más pesada que el aire.

airport A tract of land or water for the landing and takeoff of aircraft. Facilities for shelter, supply, and repair are usually found there.

aeropuerto Superficie de tierra o de agua que ha sido designada para el aterrizaje regular de aviones. En él se encuentran dependencias para el albergue, así como para suministros y reparaciones.

airway An air route marked by aids to air navigation such as beacons, radio ranges and direction-finding equipment, and along which airports are located.

ruta aérea Vía aérea demarcada por implementos de ayuda a la navegación aérea, tales como faros y equipos direccionales, y que se encuentra dentro de deterninados límites radiales. A lo largo de ella, se hallan localizados los aeropuertos.

altimeter An instrument for measuring in feet the height of the airplane above sea level.

altímetro Instrumento que mide, en pies (o metros) la altura del avión con relación al nivel del mar.

altitude The vertical distance from a given level (sea level) to an aircraft in flight.

altura Elevación a que se encuentra un avión en vuelo, con respecto a un nivel dado (nivel del mar).

attitude Position of the airplane relative to the horizon, i.e., a climbing attitude, straight-and-level attitude, etc.

posición La posición de un avión considerando la inclinación de sus ejes con respecto al horizonte: posición de ascenso, de vuelo recto, etc.

ceiling Height above ground of cloud bases.

techo Altura desde la tierra a la base de las nubes.

chart An aeronautical map showing information of use to the pilot in going from one place to another.

carta, mapa, plano Mapa que ofrece información que necesita el piloto respecto a los puntos a lo largo de un ruta aérea.

compass An instrument indicating direction.

brújula, compás Un instrumento que indica la dirección.

drag The component of the total air force on a body parallel to relative wind and opposite to thrust.

resistencia Fuerza que se opone al movimiento del avión en el aire y es opuesta al empuje.

elevation The height above sea level of a given land prominence, such as airports, mountains, etc.

elevación Altura con relación al nivel del mar.

elevators Control surfaces hinged to the horizontal stabilizer which controls the pitch of the airplane, or the position of the nose of the airplane relative to the horizon.

timón de profundidad Superficie de control abisagrada al estabilizador horizontal, que controla la posición de la proa del avión con respecto al horizonte.

engine The part of the airplane which provides power, or propulsion, to pull the airplane through the air.

motor La parte de un avión que suministra la potencia propulsora principal.

flaps Hinged or pivoted airfoils forming part of the trailing edge of the wing and used to increase lift at reduced air speeds.

flaps Plano aerodinámicos abisagrados o pivotados que forman parte del borde posterior del ala y se utilizan para aumentar la sustentación a velocidades más reducidas.

fin A vertical attachment to the tail of an aircraft which provides directional stability. Same as vertical stabilizer.

plano de deriva Superficie vertical fija que proporciona la estabilidad direccional. También se llama estabilizador vertical.

force A push or pull exerted on an object.

fuerza Acción que tiende a hacer que se mueva un cuerpo en reposo o que se detenga uno en movimiento.

fuselage The streamlined body of an airplane to which are fastened the wings and tail.

fuselaje Cuerpo del avión al cual están unidas las alas y la cola.

gravity Force toward the center of the earth.

gravedad La atracción universal de los cuerpos hacia el centro de la tierra.

hangar Building on the airport in which airplanes are stored or sheltered.

hangar Edificio u otro albergue conveniente para almacenar aviones.

knot A measure of speed, one knot being one nautical mile per hour.

nudo Unidad de velocidad igual a una milla marina por hora.

land The act of making the airplane descend, lose flying speed, and make contact with the ground or water, thus ending the flight.

aterrizar El acto de hacer descender a un avión, perder la velocidad de vuelo y tomar contacto con tierra o agua, concluyendo así el vuelo.

landing gear The understructure of an airplane which supports the airplane on land or water: wheels, skis, pontoons. Retractable gear folds up into the airplane in flight. Gear that does not retract is called "fixed."

tren de aterrizaje La estructura inferior de un aeroplano que sostiene el peso del mismo sobre tierra o agua: ruedas, esquíes, pontones. El tren de aterrizaje retráctil se pliega dentro del avión durante el vuelo. El tren que no se retrae, se llama "fijo".

lift An upward force caused by the rush of air over the wings, supporting the airplane in flight.

sustentación Fuerza de soporte inducida por la reacción dinámica del aire.

pilot Person who controls the airplane.

piloto Persona que opera los controles de un avión en vuelo.

propeller An airfoil which the engine turns to provide the thrust, pulling the airplane through the air.

hélice Una superficie aerodinámica que el motor hace girar para producir el empuje que propulsa al avión a través del aire.

radar Beamed radio waves for detecting and locating objects. The objects are "seen" on the radar screen or scope.

radar Ondas de radio especiales utilizadas para localizar y descubrir objetos. Estos objetos se "ven" en la pantalla del radar.

rudder Control surface hinged to the back of the vertical fin.

timon e dirección Superficie de control abisagrada a la parte posterior del plano de deriva.

runway A surface or area on the airport designated for airplanes to take off and land.

pista Faja de superficie pavimentada utilizada para aterrizajes y despegues.

stall The reduction of speed to the point where the wing stops producing lift.

pérdida de velocidad Pérdida de velocidad hasta el punto en que el ala deja de producir sustentación.

streamline An object shaped to make air flow smoothly around it.

perfil aerodinámico Objeto modelado en tal forma que permite que el aire se deslice a su alrededor con suavidad.

tail The part of the airplane to which the rudder and elevators are attached. The tail has vertical and horizontal stabilizers to keep the airplane from turning about its lateral axis.

cola Parte del avión en la que se encuentran el timón de dirección y el de profundidad. La cola cuenta con estabilizadores verticales y horizontales para evitar que el avión gire sobre su eje lateral.

take-off The part of the flight during which the airplane gains flying speed and becomes airborne.

despegue Acción de separarse del suelo el avión al iniciar el vuelo.

taxi To operate an airplane under its own power; other than in actual take off or landing.

carretear, rodar Maniobrar un avión en tierra bajo su propia potencia, excepto en la carrera correspondiente al despegue o al aterrizaje.

thrust Forward force.

empuje Fuerza que desplaza al avión hacia adelante.

turn Maneuver which the airplane makes in changing it direction of flight.

viraje, giro Maniobra por la cual el avión cambia de dirección.

velocity Speed.

velocidad Ligereza.

visibility Distance toward the horizon that objects can be seen and recognized. Smoke, haze, fog, and precipitation can hinder visibility.

visibilidad Distancia máxima horizontal hasta donde pueden percibirse los objetos. El humo, la neblina, la niebla y la precipitación pueden impedir la visibilidad.

wind Air motion, important to aviation because it influences flight to a certain degree.

viento Corriente de aire que resulta importante a la aviación porque influencia, hasta cierto punto, el vuelo.

wing Part of the airplane shaped like an airfoil and designed in such a way to provide lift when air flows over them.

ala Parte del avión en forma de plano aerodinámico, diseñada en forma tal de producir sustentación cuando el aire pasa por encima.

Index

About the author

Dr. Ben Millspaugh has been the director of an aviation program at Littleton High School near Denver for 22 years. The program has taught 1,833 students a full year of aviation and aerospace.

Millspaugh received a doctorate in aerospace education in 1981. He holds a commercial pilot certificate with a multiengine rating. Millspaugh has logged more than 3,800 hours and built a Fisher Classic biplane with eight students.

He has received four national honors in the field of aerospace education: 1989 A. Scott Crossfield Aerospace Teacher of the Year Award; inducted into the Crown Circle; Aerospace Education Foundation's Christa McAuliffe Award for excellence in science and mathematics in 1989; and 1990 Experimental Aircraft Association Aviation Educator of the Year. He was inducted into the Colorado Aviation Hall of Fame in 1991.

Millspaugh teaches summer aerospace workshops for teachers. The teachers earn graduate credit from Colorado State University. He is the director of the Wings of FAME organization, which recognizes teachers for outstanding work in aviation and space education.

He has written eight books including two books about the Datsun/Nissan Z-cars, prompted by his avid interest in the sports car series. Nearly 400 magazine and journal articles by Millspaugh have been published.

Other Bestsellers of Related Interest

HOMEMADE LIGHTNING:
Creative Experiments in Electrostatics
—R.A. Ford

Packed with fascinating facts, this book combines scientific history, electronics theory, and practical experiments to introduce you to the evolving science of electrostatics. The abundant illustrations and varied collection of creative, hands-on projects reveal the wide-ranging impact of electrostatics on motor design, plant growth, medicine, aerodynamics, photography, meteorology, and gravity research. 208 pages, 111 illustrations. Book No. 3576, $14.95 paperback, $23.95 hardcover

THE SPORTFLIER'S GUIDE TO RC SOARING
—Jeff Troy

If you've every visited a model airplane flying field and wondered how you could get involved in the hobby of building and flying radio-controlled (RC) airplanes, here's a great way to get started. This clear, nontechnical introduction to the popular sport of RC soaring comes complete with flying techniques. Photographs and illustrations highlight building steps and the different types of equipment. Plus, photographs of completed models make it easy for you to select and reproduce the model of your choice. 176 pages, 177 illustrations. Book No. 3519, $12.95 paperback only

HOMEMADE HOLOGRAMS:
The Complete Guide to Inexpensive,
Do-It-Yourself Holography—John Iovine

Make your own holograms, easily and inexpensively with this breakthrough book. John Iovine tells you how to produce laser-generated images plus equipment like a portable isolation table and a helium-neon laser. You'll also construct devices that can make your experiments easier and more professional, such as magnetic film holders, spatial filters, an electronic shutter, an audible electronic timer, and a laser power meter and photometer. 240 pages, 185 illustrations. Book No. 3460, $14.95 paperback, $22.95 hardcover

COMPUTERS: 49 Science Fair Projects
—Robert L. Bonnet and G. Daniel Keen

This collection of step-by-step science fair projects—using PCs and BASIC programming—challenges students ages 8 through 13 to think logically and apply the principles of scientific inquiry. Students will explore biology, physics, math, and meteorology as they develop games of chance, aircraft design tests, mathematical conversions, and much more! 190 pages, 75 illustrations. Book No. 3524, $9.95 paperback, $16.95 hardcover

OPTICAL ILLUSIONS: Puzzles, Paradoxes, and
Brain Teasers #4—Stan Gibilisco

Can you believe your eyes? No matter how trustworthy your eyes may be, they'll be teased, deceived, and dazzled with this newest addition to Gibilisco's popular series. This entertaining look at visual illusion features an intriguing collection of illustrations that deceive the human eye into seeing sizes, shapes, and motion that aren't there—or not seeing what is there! 130 pages, 107 illustrations. Book No. 3464, $8.95 paperback, $15.95 hardcover

PHYSICS FOR KIDS: 49 Easy Experiments with
Optics—Robert W. Wood

Young readers ages 8-13 will enjoy these quick and easy experiments that provide a thorough introduction to what light is, how it behaves, and how it can be put to work. Wood provides projects including: making a kaleidoscope and a periscope, an ice lens, and a pinhole camera; and learning why stars twinkle, and how a mirror works. Projects produce results often in less than 30 minutes and require only common household items to complete. 178 pages, 164 illustrations. Book No. 3402, $9.95 paperback, $16.95 hardcover

Other Bestsellers of Related Interest

PHYSICS FOR KIDS: 49 Easy Experiments with Heat—Robert W. Wood

This volume introduces thermodynamics, or the physics of heat, to students ages 8-13. By performing these safe, simple experiments, kids can begin to understand the principles of conduction, convection, and radiation. Experiments show students how to make a thermometer, make invisible ink, measure body heat, pull a wire through an ice cube, all quick, safe, and inexpensive, with results in less than 30 minutes. 160 pages, 162 illustrations. Book No. 3292, $9.95 paperback, $16.95 hardcover

''I MADE IT MYSELF'': 40 Kids' Crafts Projects—Alan and Gill Bridgewater

This easy project book will give children hours of fun crafting toys and gifts with inexpensive household materials. Children will enjoy making musical instruments, kites, dolls, cards, masks, papier-mache and painted ornaments, as well as working toys such as a wind-racer, land yacht, or moon buggy. Along with easy-to-follow instructions, each project includes scale drawings, step-by-step illustrations, and a picture of the finished item. 224 pages, 165 illustrations. Book No. 3339, $11.95 paperback, $19.95 hardcover

2583